Joe Simmer's
HEALTHY Slow Cookin'

Slow is the way!
Joe Simmer

Joe Simmer's
HEALTHY
SLOW Cookin'

CREATED BY

Michael Ledet & Richard Stewart

2 MARTINI PRESS
NEW ORLEANS
2 0 0 7

Joe enjoys a rich inner life, and sometimes intermingles imagination with reality. Any similarities to events, real or unreal, or persons, living or dead, are probably coincidental.

Although Joe is healthy, fit and strappin', he is not a health professional, and makes no health claims, express or implied.

All research conducted for *Joe Simmer's HEALTHY Slow Cookin'* has been done in fair usage.

AUGUST 24, 2007

• •

2 MARTINI PRESS

5500 Prytania Street
#616
New Orleans, LA 70115
www.2martinipress.com

Acknowledgments

JOE'S CONTRIBUTORS, illustrators, helpful friends, relatives, co-conspirators, associates, affiliated persons and spiritual advisors include Heath Vigory, Tripton Bilch, Cosimo Graham, Boland Overly, Randy Boyce, Corey C. Walsh, Jacques Allain O'Connell, Frank Beauvier, Josephine Vitracco, Emile "Unc" Richard, Anthony "Tone" Ucello, Manny Gregarian, Petra "The Greek" Opopulas, Maride duBain, José and Consuela Zima, Ethel and Judith Piaf, Colonel Jacque Rollet (Regiment de Marche, French Foreign Legion), Klaus van Zimmer, Marie Bastille, Sir Basil Simmer, Jocelyn Parker Simmer, Vitale DiFatta, Giacomo "The Spoon" Simoni, Jr., Lil' Joe Simplex, Fidel Gonzalez and family, Peter McIntosh, Purvis McSimms, Nadine (one mo' time), Selma Poché, Abe and SuSu Zimmerman, Herman and Deborah Goldblat, Father Joe Flanagan, S. J., Fabian dePeache, Melba Jo Simmer, Mathew Bloomfield Simmer III, Baxter Morgan Simmer, Britto, Siddhartha, Sri Siminanda Swamiji and Rabbi Nathan Zimmerman.

Table of Contents

*Nutritional analysis available at
www.joesimmer.com,
courtesy of Corey C. Walsh, LDN, RD*

Praise for Joe's new London show at the Tate:

"With raw power, Simmer's new work displays an organic, elemental earthiness and a healthy, age defying vitality, fused with his unique metabolic intensity—yet still redolent of the calm reserve and optimistic spunk of his past pieces. His lean abstractions transmute old world sensibleness into new age sensibilities, and convey a sprightly yet wise youthfulness, guaranteeing these new offerings great longevity."

—TRIPTON BILCH
ART CRITIC
LONDON, ENGLAND

Foreword

SO JOE SIMMER IS GOING HEALTHY—not to say that his other book was unhealthy. Well, to tell you the truth it doesn't really surprise me. I know Joe from back in the days when we shared an apartment during our medical school days.

Joe would cook all the time, with a constant stream of family and friends over at the apartment for dinner and what not. Even back then, most of his cooking was healthy in nature, being that Joe "liked the ladies" and always wanted to look his fit and virile best. As far as medical school, Joe did quite well—strait A's and such—but he was always disappointed and discouraged because they didn't teach anything about nutrition. Joe dropped out.

I left under different circumstances, and to tell you the truth, after three months in medical school, it was hard to leave Mexico and head back to Houston and work for the family vinyl siding business. But times change and years pass, and one day while entertaining a mental thought in my mind, I decided to get back into the health field and signed on with the Texas Riviera Health Spa and Salon to begin training as a personal trainer. They offered a great benefit package—major medical, 401-k, tuition re-imbursement (in fact now I am working on my Associates Degree)—and it's a great drug-free working environment.

Meanwhile, Joe went on to his own fame and fortune—art gallery showings, book signings, traipsing around the world researching recipes—and after the successes of *Joe Simmer's CREOLE Slow Cookin'* Joe caught the health bug again. While New Orleans provided Joe's culinary roots, and Creole food is pretty darn tasty, too much of it can let you pack on a few extra pounds, clog the arteries a bit, impair cognitive function and lessen ambition. For Joe, it was time to shake off the Creole yoke.

The recipes offered in this book are quintessential Joe—high in flavor and nutrition, low in saturated fat, high in fiber, devoid of trans-fats, high in antioxidants and everything else that is good for you, and of course delicious.

—HEATH VIGORY
CERTIFIED PERSONAL TRAINER

Introduction

THE PREMISE OF THIS BOOK IS SIMPLE—nutritious and delicious dishes for a healthy lifestyle, easily and conveniently prepared. This is not a "fad diet book" or "trendy weight loss program," but if you are looking to attain your ideal weight, feel better and look better, this could be the ticket—all with the ease and convenience of a slow-cooker!

Joe's recipes presented in this book are lower in saturated fat, devoid of trans-fats and refined carbohydrates, high in fiber, anti-oxidants and other age-defying nutrients, and, of course, they taste good!

The Healthy Pantry

Fresh vegetables, beans and lentils, whole grains, seafood and lean poultry are some of the stars composing the constellation of healthy slow cooking. Fresh items are, of course, best purchased fresh. Look for locally and/or organically grown produce for the best flavor and most retained nutrients. Wild caught seafood tastes better than farm raised, and again, the closer to home it is caught, the fresher it is when in gets into your pot.

When buying poultry, go for all-natural, free-range birds raised without the use of growth hormones or antibiotics.

A few healthy ingredients kept in your pantry and freezer will make preparing these tasty, nutritious recipes extra convenient. Here are Joe's suggestions:

STOCK OR BROTH—Homemade stock provides the fullest flavor, contain no added salt, generally costs the least, and is easily made in the slow-cooker (see pages 39–41). Alternatively, there are many good quality packaged broths on the market today. Look for all-natural or organic, low or reduced sodium varieties.

BEANS, PEAS AND LENTILS—These nutritional powerhouses are loaded with fiber, complex carbohydrates, protein, minerals, anti-oxidants, and other good things. Dried beans will last about a year on the shelf, and canned beans are a handy addition to many dishes. Look for all-natural or organic varieties, which are widely available.

WHOLE GRAINS—Brown rice, particularly short-grain brown and brown basmati—is a complex carbohydrate containing fiber, vitamins, minerals and a great nutty flavor. It will keep for months. Whole wheat pastry flour, kept in a sealed container in your refrigerator to avoid rancidity, is a healthier choice than white. A stock of whole wheat couscous and whole grain pasta will round out your healthy whole grain department.

HERBS AND SPICES—Buy small containers of herbs and spices so that you use them before they get old and lose their punch. Besides adding flavor, some herbs, such as rosemary, have some anti-bacterial qualities, and some spices, like turmeric and ginger provide anti-inflammatory action. A suggested stock of dried herbs and spices includes whole thyme, rubbed sage, ground black, white and cayenne pepper, whole bay leaves, ground allspice, turmeric, ginger, cinnamon, nutmeg and a pre-blended curry powder or two. Fresh herbs that are easily grown in gardens and pots include rosemary, basil, parsley, dill and cilantro.

TOMATO PRODUCTS—Tomatoes contain lycopene, a powerful anti-oxidant thought to offer many health benefits such as reducing the risk of prostate cancer, heart disease and age-related eye problems. Lycopene is much more available for absorption when tomatoes are cooked, such as in sauces, tomato paste and even catsup. Keep a couple of cans of diced tomatoes on hand, and look for all-natural or organic brands, which are readily available. Tomato paste is a great flavor enhancer and thickener for slow-cooker dishes, and is available in small cans and convenient tubes for when you just need a tablespoon or two.

For information on specific brands, grocery stores and on-line sources, check out Joe's Shopping Guide on page 131.

Slow Cooker Basics

As a means of food preparation, slow cooking has been around since the dawn of fire. A crock filled with the day's gatherings simmering in the embers of a caveman's fire was your basic pre-historic slow cooking. This morphed through time into cast iron pots over coal fires, stoves equipped with cooking wells, and other modern marvels. The disco days of the 1970's played background to the birth of today's slow-cooker.

Slow cooker technology consists of a base concealing wrap-around heating elements and a crockery insert. Food is cooked by indirect heat over a long period of time. The high setting on most slow cookers is about 300°F, low about 180°F and "keep warm" about 140°F. From manufacturer to manufacturer, and from model to model, cooker temperatures may vary somewhat, so the cooking times may vary a bit, but are pretty close. Pay attention, and after a few recipes, you will get used to the idiosyncrasies of your pot.

Slow, yet wise

For most recipes, the crock should be filled at least half way, but not much more than three-fourths, unless specified otherwise.

Refrain from putting prepared ingredients in the crock and refrigerating over night and then placing the frigid crock into the cooker base in the morning. A chilled crock will take too long to heat, risking the possibility of spoilage. Instead, refrigerate any pre-prepped ingredients in a bowl, and transfer them to the warm or room-temperature crock in the morning.

Conversely, don't put a freshly cooked crock of food in the refrigerator to cool and store. The crock takes too long to cool down. Transfer the food to other containers for cooling and storing.

Remember that removing the lid can let heat escape and increase cooking time up to 15 minutes per inspection. In general, only remove the lid to check or stir as directed.

Choosing your Cooker

Joe said it once and he will say it again: anticomplexification. That's his theory on slow-cooking and on life.

For convenience, consistency and versatility, Joe recommends a 6-quart oval shaped, programmable cooker. This size easily accommodates a pound of dried beans and is perfect for 6–8 pieces of bone-in chicken.

Considering convenience is one of the primary benefits of slow cooking, a programmable model just makes sense. If you are preparing a dish that should cook for 4 hours, but won't be back home for 6 hours, the cooker will automatically stop cooking and switch to the gentle "keep warm" setting.

For consistency, the recipes in this book have all been prepared and tested in a oval shaped, 6-quart slow-cooker.

A Convenient Truth

Joe believes that what is good for the part is good for the whole, and what is good for the whole is good for the part, and vice versa. In other words, what is good for the individual is good for the earth.

A slow cooker uses about the same amount of electricity as a 60-watt light bulb, and it doesn't heat up the kitchen as cooking in the oven or in a pot on the stove can. So, while enjoying these healthy recipes, you will know you are also contributing to a healthier environment.

Now that it's established, and generally accepted that 50 is the new 40, Joe wanted to determine the ripple effect on other ages. He conducted some research, did the math, and tabulated the results. In the final analysis, all age groups benefit as indicated in the following table:

OLD		NEW
	90 = 72	
	85 = 68	
	80 = 64	
	75 = 60	
	70 = 56	
	65 = 52	
	60 = 48	
	55 = 44	
	50 = 40	
	45 = 38	
	40 = 32	
	35 = 28	
	30 = 24	
	25 = 20	
	20 = 16	
	15 = 12	
	10 = 8	

Soups, Sauces and Stocks

SOUP AND GOOD HEALTH GO TOGETHER like ham and eggs—well, perhaps a "healthier" analogy should be employed—like beans and rice—but that's another chapter. Soups are an easy and excellent way to incorporate all sorts of healthy ingredients into delicious and easy one-dish meals. Stock is an important part of most soups, and in many cases, the better the stock, the better the soup. Check out the stock recipes at the end of this chapter. They are easy, and can be kept on hand in the freezer for months. If you only want to make one stock, and you are not a strict vegetarian, choose chicken—the universal stock.

Red Lentil Soup with Carrots and Celery
Minestrone
Tomato Basil Soup
Mushroom Barley Soup
Vegetable Curry Potage
Turkey Vegetable Soup
Chicken Noodle Soup
Chicken Posole Soup
Cabbage Soup with Caraway
Split Pea Soup with Smoked Turkey
Navy Bean Soup with Turkey Tasso
Thick and Chunky Tomato Sauce
Vegetable Stock
Chicken Stock
Seafood Stock

Nutritional analysis available at
www.joesimmer.com,
courtesy of Corey C. Walsh, LDN, RD

Red Lentil Soup with Carrots and Celery

SERVES 6–8

THESE LENTILS TURN A WARM GOLDEN HUE when cooked, but when purchased, their color may be described as sort of pinkish red, or maybe spring salmon, or sautéed shrimp or perhaps ripened peach or possibly peeled papaya—thus the name. They require no soaking and cook quite quickly. Red lentils boast a particularly savory flavor. People will swear chicken stock provides the background flavor for this soup, where the only liquid in this recipe is plain ole water.

3 tablespoons extra virgin olive oil	1 teaspoon dried thyme
2 cups chopped onion	½ teaspoon sage
1 cup celery cut in ¼ inch diagonal slices, about 3 stalks	½ teaspoon black pepper
	½ teaspoon white pepper
1½ cups carrots, cut in ¼ inch diagonal slices, about 3 or 4 medium carrots	¼ teaspoon cayenne pepper, or to taste
½ cup finely chopped shallot	1 lb red lentils, rinsed
1 tablespoon minced garlic	7 cups water
3 bay leaves, crushed	1 tablespoon balsamic vinegar
	1 tablespoon tamari sauce
	1 teaspoon salt, or to taste

In a large skillet set over a medium-high heat, heat the olive oil and sauté the chopped onion for 5–7 minutes, or until translucent. Add the celery, carrots, shallots, garlic, bay leaves, thyme, sage and peppers. Cook for 2 minutes, stirring once or twice.

Transfer the contents of the skillet to the slow cooker along with the rinsed lentils and water. Cover and cook on low for 7–8 hours or high for 3½–4 hours. Add the balsamic vinegar, tamari and salt. Stir to mix and cook an additional 10–15 minutes.

Chef's Notes: *Red lentils practically disintegrate when cooked, giving this soup a creamy, rich texture.*

WINE SUGGESTION: A Spanish Tempranillo if you're looking for red, or a simple white Burgundy like a Mâcon-Villages

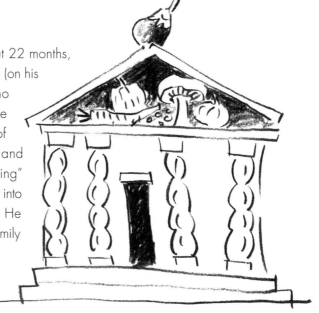

During a period of about 22 months, when Joe's second cousin (on his father's side) Giacomo Simoni had a lot of free time on his hands—courtesy of the federal government and due to a "misunderstanding" with the IRS—he really got into genealogical research. He was trying to locate the family of a "business associate" who suddenly moved back to Sicily, with no forwarding address.

After dispensing with that business, he started researching his own family's past, tracing it back to the year LXXIIV and an ancestor named Jovinianus Flavius Simplex. Uncle Jovinianus, a successful merchant and member of the senate, operated Rome's first and finest fruit and vegetable emporium. His descendents followed in his footsteps, growing and distributing produce all over Italy and beyond. Several scions landed in New Jersey, and one migrated to New Orleans around 1905, settling in the suburb of Chalmette, where he operated a truck farm, specializing in vine-ripened Creole tomatoes.

Minestrone

MINESTRONE, THE FAMOUS and hearty Italian vegetable soup varies from region to region, and even from household to household—kind of like gumbo in Louisiana. Most contain onion, carrots, celery and tomatoes, with additional regional or seasonal vegetables. All use water instead of stock, although some may include pancetta or some other pork product. This one is a meat-free vegetarian version, passed on to Joe from his cousin Guido's father Giacomo Simoni, who, after his divorce, liquidated all his assets in New Jersey, moved to an ashram in Oregon and became a strict vegan. He refused to eat anything that would kill, harm or degrade another sentient being. With all due respect, Joe likes to garnish his minestrone with a bit of grated Reggiano Parmesan, sprinkled on at the table.

3 tablespoons extra virgin olive oil

2 cups chopped onion

2 tablespoons minced garlic

1 tablespoon minced fresh rosemary

1 teaspoon whole dried thyme

1 teaspoon whole dried basil

1 teaspoon black pepper

⅛ teaspoon cayenne pepper

2 tablespoons tomato paste

3 stalks celery, sliced ¼ inch thick, about 1½ cups

3 leeks, trimmed and washed, cut in half lengthwise and cross-cut into ¼ inch thick slices, about 3 cups

3 medium carrots, sliced into ¼ inch rounds

½ small head green cabbage, cut into 1 inch squares, about 4 cups

2 cups diced fresh tomato, or one 14½ ounce can diced tomatoes

6 cups water

3 bay leaves

1 15 ounce can cannelloni beans or great northern white beans, drained

1 15 ounce can chickpeas (garbanzo beans), drained

3 small zucchini, trimmed and cut in half lengthwise and sliced into ¼ inch slices

1 cup small whole wheat pasta, such as ditalini, orecchiette, small shells or elbows

| ¼ cup chopped flat leaf parsley | Freshly grated Reggiano Parmesan cheese, if desired |
| 1 teaspoon salt, or to taste | |

Heat the oil in a large skillet set over a medium-high heat. Add the chopped onion, cook and stir for 5 minutes or until tender and lightly browned. Add the garlic, rosemary, thyme, basil, black pepper, cayenne pepper and tomato paste. Stir well to mix and cook for another 3–5 minutes, stirring, scraping up and stirring back in any tomato paste that might stick to the bottom of the pan.

Transfer the contents of the skillet to the crock. Use a little of the water to loosen any bits stuck to the bottom of the pan and add it to the crock along with the next 7 ingredients. Cover and cook for 6 hours on low or 3 hours on high. If cooking on low, switch to high and add the beans, zucchini, pasta, parsley and salt. Stir to mix. Cover and cook on high for 1–1½ hours or until the pasta is done and the zucchini is tender. If possible, stir once during the last hour of cooking.

Serve in large soup bowls with slices of whole wheat garlic bread—made with olive oil, not butter. Pass around a bowl of grated Parmesan to sprinkle onto the bowls of minestrone, if desired.

• • • • • • • • • • • • •

Chef's Notes: *You can vary the beans in this recipe to your liking, and if you wish, you may use chicken stock instead of water.*

• • • • • • • • • • • • •

WINE SUGGESTION: Italian, of course. For red a Chianti Classico, for white a fuller bodied Pinot Grigio. If you stray from the Italian theme, a California Viognier would be nice.

Tomato Basil Soup

SERVES 6–8

SWEET BASIL IS SO EASY TO GROW and will thrive all summer in your garden. Adding fresh-picked flavor to many a dish, it has natural affinity for tomatoes—and vine ripened tomatoes are also plentiful during the summer months. This soup is easy, elegant, nutritious and delicious—and can be enjoyed hot right out of the crock, or chilled.

1 tablespoon extra virgin olive oil

3 cups chopped onion

½ cup chopped shallot

1 tablespoon minced garlic

1 teaspoon dried basil

½ teaspoon black pepper

½ teaspoon white pepper

1 pinch cayenne pepper, or to taste

½ teaspoon dry mustard

2 tablespoons tomato paste

3 cups chicken stock (page 40) or broth, or vegetable stock (page 39) or broth

18 medium-sized fresh Roma tomatoes, about 3½ lbs

½ cup chopped fresh basil

1 tablespoon balsamic vinegar

½ teaspoon salt, or to taste

FOR GARNISH:

Thick, Greek style yogurt

Fresh lemon wedges

Chopped fresh basil

Heat the olive oil in a large skillet set over a medium-high heat. Add the chopped onion and sauté, stirring occasionally for 6–8 minutes. Stir in the chopped shallot, minced garlic, dried basil, black pepper, white pepper, cayenne pepper, dry mustard and tomato paste and cook for 1 minute. Transfer the contents of the pan to the crock. Deglaze the pan with the stock or broth and pour it into the crock.

Cut the Roma tomatoes in quarters and add them to the crock along with the chopped fresh basil, vinegar and salt. Stir, cover and cook on high for 3 hours or low for 6 hours.

Ladle the soup into a blender, in batches if necessary, and purée. Serve in large bowls, stirring in the yogurt, lemon juice and fresh basil garnishes at the table if desired.

● ●

Chef's Notes: *Some people don't like the combination of tomato and dairy products, but if all your diners are of the opposite persuasion, you can add the yogurt (about ½ cup) during the puréeing process.*

● ●

WINE SUGGESTION: Something light, like a Pinot Grigio.

Mushroom Barley Soup

SERVES 6–8

THIS HEALTH FOOD STORE DELI CLASSIC, enjoyed by northeastern intellectu-
als, hippies and philosophy professors for years, has finally made it out of the
New England co-op and into the all-American crock pot. What a sellout!

Joe's jazzed it up a bit, adding more high-brow mushrooms and a liberal dose
of seasoning, but it's still as comforting and profound as a crisp New Hampshire
autumn afternoon, thoughtfully enjoyed while resting your suede-patched elbow on
the rolled-down window of your green Volvo station wagon.

½ **ounce dried porcini mushrooms**

1 **cup boiling water**

2 **tablespoons extra virgin
olive oil**

2½ **cups chopped onion**

½ **cup finely chopped shallot**

1 **cups ¼ inch sliced celery**

½ **cup finely chopped carrot**

1 **tablespoon minced garlic**

3 **bay leaves, crushed**

½ **teaspoon black pepper, or
to taste**

⅛ **teaspoon cayenne pepper,
or to taste**

1 **teaspoon salt, or to taste**

¼ **cup chopped parsley**

¼ **teaspoon rubbed sage**

2 **tablespoons chopped fresh
rosemary**

½ **teaspoon dried thyme**

½ **pound sliced baby Portobello mushrooms**

3 **ounces shitake mushrooms,
trimmed and sliced**

1 **cup hulled barley or Scotch
barley, rinsed**

6 **cups vegetable stock (page
39) or low-sodium veg-
etable broth; or 6 cups
chicken stock (page 40) or
low-sodium chicken broth**

½ **cup dry white wine**

Place the dried porcinis in a small bowl and pour on the boiling water. Cover
and allow to soak while preparing the other ingredients.

Heat the oil in a large skillet set over a medium-high heat. Add the onion,
shallot, celery, and carrot and cook, stirring occasionally, for 10–12 minutes,
or until some of the onion begins to brown a bit. Add the garlic, bay leaves,

black pepper, cayenne pepper and salt and cook for 1 minute. Stir in the parsley, sage, rosemary and thyme, and remove the pan from the heat.

Remove the porcinis from the soaking liquid, rinse them and finely chop. Strain the soaking liquid through a coffee filter or a piece of cheesecloth and add it to the crock, along with the chopped porcinis, sliced baby Portobello mushrooms, sliced shitakes and rinsed barley. Distribute the contents of the skillet over all the ingredients in the slow cooker, and gently pour in the stock or broth. Rinse out the skillet with the wine and add it to the crock. Cover and cook on high for 3–4 hours or low for 6–8 hours.

• •

Chef's Notes: *Hulled barley is usually available at natural food markets, and is higher in fiber and nutrients than brown rice, whole wheat or oats. The more common pearled barley is more refined and not as nutritious or chewy. It cooks faster, so if you use it, go for the shorter cooking times.*

• •

WINE SUGGESTION: An earthy red Côtes du Rhône or a fruity Beaujolais.

Vegetable Curry Potage

SERVES 6-8

2 tablespoons extra virgin
   olive oil
2 cups coarsely chopped onion
16 ounces fresh (trimmed off
   the cob) or frozen corn
2 tablespoons whole-wheat
   pastry flour
¼ cup water
1 cup coarsely chopped celery
1 cup coarsely chopped red
   bell pepper
3 cups russet potatoes, peeled
   and cut into 1-inch cubes
2 tablespoons chopped
   parsley
1 lb frozen lima beans

1 tablespoon fresh ground
   black pepper
1 teaspoon salt
1½ cups chicken stock (page 40)
   or broth
½ teaspoon dried ground
   thyme
1 lb frozen green peas
2 tablespoons chopped fresh
   basil
2 tablespoons curry powder
Water as needed
1 tablespoon thick Greek style
   yogurt per serving
   (optional)
1 teaspoon shredded fresh
   basil per serving (optional)

Heat the olive oil in a large skillet set over a medium-high heat. Sauté the onions and corn, sprinkled with the flour for 10–12 minutes, stirring frequently until the onions turn soft and the corn starts to stick to the skillet. Transfer contents of skillet to the slow cooker. Deglaze the skillet with ¼ cup water and add it to the slow cooker.

Add the celery, bell pepper, potatoes, parsley, lima beans, black pepper, salt, ground thyme and chicken stock to the slow cooker. Stir well. Cover and cook on high for 3–4 hours or low for 6–8 hours. Add green peas and basil and a little water if needed. Stir and cook for another hour.

Transfer the contents of the slow cooker to a large bowl to cool. When cool enough to handle, stir in the curry powder. Place mixture in a food processor or blender and process or blend, adding water as needed to achieve the consistency of heavy cream (you may have to do this in batches). Serve the potage with a garnish of thick yogurt and fresh basil if desired.

Turkey Vegetable Soup

SERVES 6–8

8 cups chicken stock (page 40) or broth

½ head cabbage, diced

3 small carrots, sliced

3 small turnips, scrubbed and diced

1 14½ ounce can diced tomatoes

2 cups chopped onion

3 small leeks, white and light green parts, chopped

3 bay leaves

1 teaspoon salt, or to taste

1 teaspoon black pepper

⅛ teaspoon cayenne pepper, or to taste

1 skinless turkey thigh, bone-in, about 2½ lbs

½ cup chopped parsley

1 tablespoon balsamic vinegar

Place all the ingredients except the turkey thigh, chopped parsley and balsamic vinegar in the crock and stir to mix. Place the turkey thigh on top, cover and cook on high for 5 hours, or until vegetables are tender and turkey is cooked through. Remove the turkey, and when cooled enough to handle, remove the bone and cut the meat into bite sized pieces. Return it to the crock along with the chopped parsley and balsamic vinegar. Adjust the seasoning and cook for an additional 15–30 minutes.

• • • • • • •

WINE SUGGESTION: A crisp Sauvignon Blanc.

Chicken Noodle Soup

ABE ZIMMERMAN AND HIS WIFE SUSU both worked as Wall Street investment bankers, their long days filled with deal closings, hedge fund managers, leveraged buy-outs, hostile takeovers, power lunches, share-holder meetings, flying to Washington to lobby senators, and other stresses of the trade. Abe routinely contracted at least four head colds and one bout with the flu every year for which he kept a stash of exotic antibiotics.

A distant relative of Joe's (on his father's mother's side), Abe always thought of the Simmers as a bunch of ne'er do well schleps and un-ambitious schmucks. His perception changed when he read one of Joe's books, and quickly calculated its earning potential. He began to look upon Joe as a khoshev, and admired his chutzpah. He was further impressed after running into Joe in the Miami airport on his way to visit SuSu's parents, Herman and Deborah Goldblat. Joe was just leaving town after meeting with the Gonzales family researching some Cuban black bean recipes. Noticing Abe's red, watery eyes and runny nose, (and happy he was no longer regarded as chopped liver) Joe offered him a few healthy, healing recipes - including his new traditional chicken noodle soup. Between coughing fits, Abe thanked Joe profusely, noting it reminded him of his dear mother's recipe, only not so schmaltzy, and christened it "the chosen soup". It's a little more work than opening a can of Campbell's, but what's the point of life without a little suffering?

1 **tablespoon extra virgin olive oil**	2 **cups ¼-inch sliced carrots**
3 **cups chopped onion**	8 **cups chicken stock, page 40, or broth**
2 **cups ¼-inch sliced celery**	4 **skinless bone-in chicken breasts, about 3 lbs**
1 **tablespoon minced garlic**	¼ **pound whole wheat fettuccini**
1½ **teaspoons thyme**	1 **cup thinly sliced green onions**
1 **teaspoon black pepper, or to taste**	⅓ **cup chopped parsley**
Pinch of cayenne pepper, or to taste	
½ **teaspoon salt, or to taste**	
3 **bay leaves, crushed**	

Heat the olive oil in a large skillet set over a medium-high heat. Add the onion and celery and sauté for 4–5 minutes, or until slightly softened. Stir in the garlic, thyme, black pepper, cayenne, salt and bay leaves and cook for 1 minute. Transfer the contents of the pan to the crock and stir in the carrots and stock. Put the chicken breasts on top, cover and cook on high for 3–4 hours or low for 6–7 hours.

Remove the chicken from the slow cooker and set aside to cool a bit. Break the fettuccini into 2-inch lengths and cook according to package directions. Drain and add to the crock along with the green onions and parsley, and cook for an additional 15 minutes on high or 30 minutes on low. When the chicken is cool enough to handle, remove the bones and cut the meat into bite-sized pieces. Return the chicken meat to the crock and allow it to re-heat. Adjust the seasoning and serve.

• •

Chef's Notes: *Whole-wheat pasta varies greatly in quality and taste. Look for an organic, Italian-made brand.*

• •

WINE SUGGESTION: An un-oaked Chardonnay, French or American, or a fruity Pinot Noir. For the traditionalist (or orthodox), a small tumbler of Mogen David Concord red would be kosher.

Chicken Posole Soup

SERVES 6

DURING HIS STINT IN THE PEACE CORP, Joe spent some time supervising an irrigation project in a small village in western Mexico. Corn, also known as maize, filled most of the fields, much of which was processed into posole, also known as hominy. The whole kernels are soaked in water and lime, which loosens the hard outer husk and leaves a distinct Mexican flavor. It's often cooked in a rich soup for special festive occasions. Joe became such a fan that the locals started calling him "Hominy Joe". Here Joe replaces the traditional pork with skinless chicken thighs for a healthier version.

12 ounces dried posole, about 2 cups	1 tablespoon mild chili powder
3 cups water	1 teaspoon ground cumin
6 cups chicken stock, page 40, or broth	1 teaspoon oregano
1 tablespoon extra virgin olive oil	½ teaspoon salt, or to taste
2 cups chopped onion	1½–2 pounds boneless, skinless chicken thighs
1 cup chopped poblano pepper or green bell pepper	Chopped fresh cilantro
½ cup chopped carrot	Chopped fresh jalapeno peppers
2 tablespoons minced garlic	Shredded green cabbage
3 tablespoons minced fresh jalapeno pepper	Fresh lime wedges
	Thinly sliced radishes

Rinse the posole and place it in a 2 or 3 quart non-reactive saucepan. Add the three cups of water and soak overnight. When you are ready to start cooking, drain the posole and add the chicken stock to the saucepan. Bring the pot to a boil over a medium heat, cover and remove it from the heat.

Heat the olive oil in a large skillet set over a medium-high heat. Add the chopped onion, poblano or green bell pepper and carrot and cook for 10 minutes, stirring occasionally. Stir in the garlic, jalapeño, chili powder, cumin, oregano and salt and cook for 1 minute. Transfer the contents of the pan to the crock, along with the posole and stock, and stir to mix. Place the chicken thighs on top, cover and cook on high for 2–3 hours or low for 4–6 hours, or until the chicken is done and the posole is tender but still chewy. Remove the chicken thighs, chop or shred, and stir back into the soup.

Serve in large bowls, passing around garnishes including chopped cilantro, chopped fresh jalapeño, shredded cabbage, radishes and lime wedges.

• •

Chef's Notes: *Posole is available from many natural food stores, Latin markets and on-line vendors. It is very popular in the southwestern United States, especially New Mexico.*

• •

WINE SUGGESTION: Skip the wine and have a cold Negro Modelo.

Cabbage Soup with Caraway

SERVES 6

FEW FOODS SCREAM HEALTH LIKE CABBAGE. A cruciferous vegetable, it contains phytochemicals thought to have great cancer fighting properties, a good amount of fiber, and is low in calories. Quite versatile culinarily, it is easy to prepare and is abundant and inexpensive.

3 tablespoons extra virgin olive oil

2 cups chopped onion

1 cup finely chopped shallot

3 leeks, white and light green parts only, cut in half lengthwise and thinly sliced into half-rounds, about 3–3½ cups

3 small red potatoes, peeled and cut into ½ inch dice

2 tablespoons minced garlic

1 teaspoon caraway seeds

1 teaspoon black pepper

1 bayleaf

½ head green cabbage, shredded, about 5–6 cups

4 cups chicken stock (page 40) or low-sodium broth

1 teaspoon salt, or to taste

¼ cup white vermouth

½ cup chopped parsley

Roquefort cheese, crumbled, for garnish (optional)

Heat the oil in a large skillet set over a medium heat. Add the chopped onion, finely chopped shallot and sliced leeks and cook for 8–10 minutes, stirring often, until softened but not browned. Stir in the diced potatoes and garlic and cook for an additional 5 minutes, stirring often. Stir in the caraway seeds, black pepper and bay leaf and transfer the contents of the pan to the slow cooker, along with the shredded cabbage and chicken stock. Cover and cook for 3–3½ hours on high or 6–7 hours on low.

Stir the soup with a wire whip and mash up some of the diced potatoes to thicken the broth. Remove the bay leaf and stir in the salt, white vermouth and parsley, and cook for an additional 10–15 minutes. Serve in large bowls

with crumbled Roquefort cheese to sprinkle on top, if desired. Crisp whole grain garlic bread would make a delicious accompaniment.

• •

Chef's Notes: *In simple dishes like this, it is worth the effort of using a rich homemade chicken stock, though you will still get tasty results with a good quality packaged broth.*

• •

WINE SUGGESTION: Any Riesling, dry or off-dry, or a nice Tavel rosé.

Split Pea Soup
with Smoked Turkey

THE VAN ZIMMER BRANCH OF JOE'S FAMILY would be proud of this blend of Netherlands tradition and California sensibility.

1 **lb green split peas, rinsed**	1 **teaspoon black pepper**
6 **cups chicken stock (page 40)**	¼ **teaspoon cayenne pepper,**
2 **cups finely chopped onion**	**or to taste**
¾ **cup chopped carrot**	1 **smoked turkey thigh,**
½ **cup chopped celery**	**about 1 lb**
1 **tablespoon minced garlic**	2 **tablespoons red wine**
3 **bay leaves, crushed**	**vinegar**
1½ **teaspoons dried thyme**	1–2 **teaspoons salt, or to taste**

Combine the rinsed peas, chicken stock, finely chopped onion, chopped carrot, chopped celery, minced garlic, bay leaves, thyme and peppers in the slow cooker. Stir to mix. Remove the skin and any visible fat from the smoked turkey thigh, and place it in the center of the crock, on top of everything else. Cover and cook on high for 3–4 hours or low for 6–8 hours.

Remove the turkey thigh and set aside to cool a bit. Add the red wine vinegar and salt, stir the soup well with a wire whip and adjust the seasoning. Strip the turkey meat from the bones and coarsely chop. Return the meat to the crock and cook for an additional 10 or 15 minutes.

Serve in large bowls with toasted whole grain pumpernickel bread and perhaps a tossed salad dressed with a simple vinaigrette.

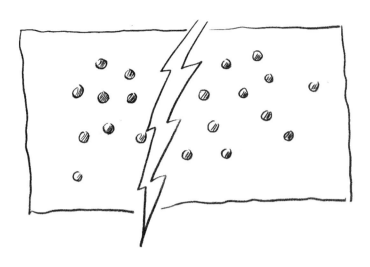

• •

Chef's Notes: *When selecting smoked turkey, look for a naturally smoked, free-range product, available at most natural food markets. They are usually less salty, contain no added nitrites, and the natural smoke flavor leaves no "artificial" aftertaste.*

• •

WINE SUGGESTION: An off-dry Riesling works well with the smoky flavor, and especially well if you are a bit heavy-handed with the cayenne.

Navy Bean Soup with Turkey Tasso

J OE'S FAMOUS LOUISIANA STATE SENATE BEAN SOUP from his Creole Slow Cookin' book drew fans from every political persuasion—a true bi-partisan dish. With health concerns mounting in the House, and his constituency demanding a reworked, lighter version, Joe went back into committee and pounded out this compromise recipe. Some of the more conservative Senators quipped " this is so healthy it could be called California State Senate Bean Soup".

1 lb dried navy beans	1 tablespoon minced garlic
8 cups water	1 teaspoon salt, or to taste
½ lb turkey tasso	½ teaspoon white pepper
3 bay leaves	¼ teaspoon cayenne pepper
3 tablespoons extra virgin olive oil	1 tablespoon white wine vinegar
2 cups finely chopped onion	

Combine the beans and the 8 cups of water in a large non-reactive saucepan, cover and soak overnight in the refrigerator. When you are ready to cook, bring the pot to a boil, remove it from the heat and cover while preparing the other ingredients.

Place the beans and their soaking liquid, the turkey tasso and bay leaves in the crock. Cook on high for 3 hours or low for 6 hours, or until beans are tender. Remove the bay leaves and discard. Remove the turkey tasso, cool and chop into an approximately ¼-inch dice. Remove ¼ cup of the beans and mash them into a smooth paste.

Heat the olive oil in a large skillet. Add the chopped onions and sauté over a medium-high heat, stirring frequently, for 10 minutes until soft and lightly browned. Add the garlic, salt and peppers and cook one minute more.

Add this to the crock along with the chopped turkey tasso, mashed beans and vinegar. Continue cooking on high for ½ hour or low for 1 hour.

• •

Chef's Notes: *Check out the Shopping Guide, page 131, if you have trouble finding turkey tasso.*

• •

WINE SUGGESTION: Try a white Albariño from Spain, or a medium bodied red Zinfandel.

Thick and Chunky Tomato Sauce

MAKES ABOUT 5 QUARTS

Use this easy, delicious and nutritious sauce over whole wheat pasta, or with meatballs, meatloaf, chicken or other dishes. Tomatoes are a rich source of vitamins A, C, calcium and lycopene.

3 **tablespoons extra virgin olive oil**	⅛ **teaspoon cayenne pepper, or to taste**
5 **cups chopped onion**	2 **29 ounce cans crushed tomatoes**
2 **tablespoons minced garlic**	
1 **teaspoon dried basil**	2 **29 ounce cans diced tomatoes**
½ **teaspoon dried oregano**	
½ **teaspoon black pepper**	½ **teaspoon salt, or to taste**
¼ **cup tomato paste**	1 **cup chopped fresh basil**

Heat the olive oil in a large skillet over medium heat. Add the onions and cook, stirring often for 15 minutes, until softened and lightly browned. Stir in the garlic, dried basil, dried oregano, black pepper, tomato paste and cayenne pepper. Cook an additional 3 minutes.

Transfer the contents of the skillet into the crock. Pour one can of the diced tomatoes, un-drained, into the skillet, stir to deglaze and transfer to the crock. Add the other un-drained can of diced tomatoes to the crock along with the 2 cans of crushed tomatoes and stir to mix. Cover and cook on high for 5–6 hours or low for 10–12 hours, stirring once during the cooking process if possible.

Adjust the seasoning, add salt if necessary, and stir in the chopped fresh basil.

• •

Chef's Notes: *This sauce freezes well, and it's handy to keep a few pints in the freezer so you can quickly whip up healthy and tasty meals.*

Vegetable Stock

USE THIS IN PLACE OF CHICKEN STOCK for much lighter flavor or for a totally vegetarian dish.

3 quarts chopped vegetables (and vegetable scraps and trimmings), including onions, garlic, squash, carrots, celery, mushrooms, peas, corn, corn cobs, parsley, green beans, beets, bell peppers, scallions, green onions, shallots, fresh basil or other herbs. A small amount of tomato may be added, unless you want a strong tomato flavor. Avoid broccoli, cauliflower, cabbage and Brussels sprouts, as they can overpower the stock with their strong flavor.

3 quarts water, approximately

Place the vegetables in the slow cooker and add enough water to fill the crock to about one inch from the top. Cover and cook on high for 4–5 hours or low for 8–10 hours. Strain the finished stock into a bowl or pot, pressing the solids with the back of a spoon to extract as much liquid as possible.

Place the stock in the refrigerator and allow it to thoroughly chill. The stock can be held refrigerated for 3–4 days, or frozen for 6 months.

• •

Chef's Notes: *The flavor will vary a bit depending on your selection of vegetables.*

• •

Chicken Stock

MAKES ABOUT 2½ QUARTS

SIMPLE AND FLAVORFUL, this stock is fat free and contains no carbohydrates. It's so rich in flavor, you could dilute it with an equal amount of water and it would still deliver more punch than packaged broths—and with less sodium. For the best flavor, look for free-range, all-natural chicken.

5 lbs bone-in chicken parts (backs, thighs, drumsticks and/or wings)

1 medium onion, peeled and cut into eighths

1 carrot, scrubbed and trimmed, cut into 1-inch pieces

1 celery stalk, scrubbed and trimmed, cut into 1-inch pieces

8 cups water

Place all the ingredients in the slow cooker. The amount of water may vary somewhat, but 8 cups is about right for a 6 quart oval shaped crock. The water should be about an inch from the top. Cover and cook on high for 5–6 hours or low for 10–12 hours. Strain the finished stock into a bowl or pot, and press the solids with the back of a spoon to extract as much of the liquid as possible.

Place the bowl or pot in the refrigerator and chill thoroughly. Remove the solidified fat from the top and discard. Refrigerated, the stock can be held for 3–4 days, or for 6 months frozen.

● ●

Chef's Notes: *Although mainly intended for chicken recipes, this is considered by many as the universal stock, and can enhance the flavor of seafood, bean, lentil and vegetable dishes also.*

For a darker color and deeper flavor, place the chicken parts, onion, carrot and celery on a sheet pan and roast in a 400° oven for about 45 minutes, or until well browned, before placing in the slow cooker.

● ●

Seafood Stock

1 tablespoon olive oil

1 medium onion, sliced

3 peeled garlic cloves, smashed

2 lbs mild, white fish (backbones leftover from cutting filets are good)

1 lb shrimp heads and shells

1 lb small blue crabs, cleaned

1 carrot, scrubbed and trimmed, cut into 1-inch pieces

1 celery stalk, scrubbed and trimmed, cut into 1-inch pieces

1 teaspoon black peppercorns

1 teaspoon fresh lemon juice

3 quarts water

Heat the olive oil in a small pan and sauté the onion and garlic over medium heat until softened, about 5 minutes. Transfer the contents of the pan to the slow cooker and add all remaining ingredients. Adjust the amount of water so that the crock in filled to about an inch from the top, cover and cook on high for 4–5 hours or low for 8–10 hours.

Strain the finished stock into a bowl or pot, pressing the solids with the back of a spoon to extract as much of the liquid as possible. Chill thoroughly. Skim any fat from the top.

Stock can be held in the refrigerator for 3 or 4 days, or frozen for about 6 months.

• •

Chef's Notes: *For a lighter, more delicately flavored stock, use four pounds of fish and omit the shellfish. You may also use fish and only shrimp, or all shellfish. 2 lbs of head-on shrimp will yield about 1 lb of heads and shells for stock.*

• •

Beans, Peas and Lentils

THE CONNECTION BETWEEN BEANS AND HEALTH has been well established in modern nutritional and longevity communities. Folklore surrounding an ancient middle eastern bean dish suggests that daily consumption will result in eternal life. This has been neither proved nor disproved.

The only remaining question is: What is the best way to cook beans to preserve their health-giving magic? Consider the following diagram:

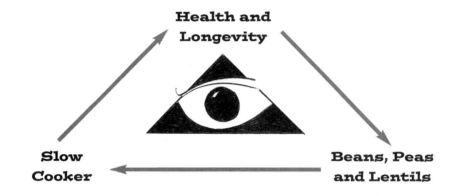

Clearly, the slow cooker controls a vital angle in this equilateral triangle of health and longevity.

Butter Beans with Caramelized Onions
José Zima's Mexican Health Beans
Brown Beans with Turkey Tasso
Lentils with Eggplant
French Foreign Legion Lentils
White Beans with White Vermouth
Red Beans with Smoked Turkey
Vegetarian Chili
Dal

*Nutritional analysis available at
www.joesimmer.com,
courtesy of Corey C. Walsh, LDN, RD*

Butter Beans with Caramelized Onions

SERVES 6

THOUGH THESE BEANS ARE BIG, they tend to cook rather quickly and there is no need for soaking.

2 **tablespoons extra virgin olive oil**	1 **teaspoon dried whole thyme**
4 **cups sliced onion (cut onions in half lengthwise and slice into ¼ inch thick semi-circles)**	3 **bay leaves, crushed**
	5 **cups chicken stock (page 40) or broth**
1 **tablespoon tomato paste**	1 **lb dried butter beans (large limas)**
1 **tablespoon minced garlic**	1 **teaspoon salt, or to taste**
1 **teaspoon black pepper**	1 **tablespoon balsamic vinegar**
¼ **teaspoon cayenne pepper, or to taste**	¼ **cup chopped parsley**

Heat the olive oil in a large pan set over a medium-high heat. Add the onion slices and cook, stirring frequently until deep golden brown, about 15–20 minutes. Stir in the tomato paste, and then add the garlic, black pepper, cayenne pepper, thyme and bay leaves. Cook for 1 minute. Transfer the contents of the pan to the crock. Use a little of the stock to deglaze the pan and add it to the crock along with the rest of the stock and the butter beans. Stir to mix, cover and cook on high for 3–3½ hours or low for 6–7 hours or until beans are tender. Stir in the salt, vinegar and parsley.

● ●

WINE SUGGESTION: The deep flavor of the caramelized onions coupled with the rich texture of the butter beans let this dish stand up to a big, structured Cabernet Sauvignon or Bordeaux. If you want white, go for a heavier, full bodied California Chardonnay.

Slimmer with Simmer

José Zima's Mexican Health Beans

AFTER TWO YEARS IN NEW ORLEANS, Joe's friend José Zima noticed he had packed on a few pounds. Even his long days of hauling seal-tab shingles up ladders and herding his raucous crew of roofers couldn't make caloric compensation for his new-found addiction to French Fry Po-Boys with Roast Beef Gravy, Soufflé Potatoes with Béarnaise and other rich local treats. Early one morning while picking up some k-style gutters and a Chinese hat vent, he heard some of the guys at the Home Depot looking his way and muttering something about "el hombre gordo". Later, when he began having a hard time seeing his feet, he overheard his crew putting money in the pool betting when he would miss the top rung and plunge to his death. José knew it was time for a change. He called Joe.

Not wanting to lose his new amigo to an accident or a heart attack, Joe hand delivered hot samples of his new healthy test recipes to José every evening. José really got into the whole health thing and came up with this recipe.

1 **lb dried black beans**	1½ **teaspoon ground cumin**
6 **cups water**	½ **teaspoon dried whole**
3 **tablespoons extra virgin**	**oregano**
olive oil, divided	3 **bay leaves, crushed**
2 **cups chopped white onion**	2 **tablespoons minced garlic**
1 **cup chopped green bell**	2 **tablespoons fresh lime juice**
pepper	½ **teaspoon salt, or to taste**
1 **cup chopped red bell pepper**	
1 **cup chopped yellow bell**	**GARNISHES (optional):**
pepper	**Chopped cilantro**
2 **tablespoons minced**	**Lime wedges**
Jalapeno pepper, seeds	**Chopped Jalapeno peppers**
removed before mincing	

Rinse the beans and place them in a large, non-reactive saucepan, and pour in the water. Cover and refrigerate at least 8 hours or overnight. When ready to cook, place the saucepan over a medium heat, bring it to a gentle boil, remove from the heat, cover and set aside while you are preparing the other ingredients,

Heat 2 tablespoons of the olive oil in a large skillet set over a medium-high heat. Add the chopped onion, bell peppers and jalapeno pepper and cook, stirring occasionally, for about 6–8 minutes. Stir in the cumin, oregano and bay leaves.

Transfer the contents of the pan to the crock and stir in the beans and their soaking liquid. Cover and cook on high for 2½–3½ hours or low for 5–7 hours, or until the beans are tender.

Heat the remaining tablespoon of olive oil in a small pan over a medium heat and stir in the 2 tablespoons of minced garlic. Cook, stirring constantly for a few minutes until the garlic is evenly golden brown, and immediately stir it into the beans in the crock. Stir in the lime juice and salt.

Serve in large bowls, or on plates over steamed brown rice, with small bowls of chopped cilantro, fresh lime wedges and chopped fresh jalapeno pepper for garnish, if desired.

• •

Chef's Notes: *If red and yellow bell peppers are not available, just use and equal amount of green and red, or green and yellow, or all green.*

• •

WINE SUGGESTION: If you are in the mood for red, try a medium to full bodied Zinfandel. Most whites, from Riesling to Viognier to Pinot Grigio would complement this nicely, as would most Rosés.

Brown Beans
with Turkey Tasso

SERVES 6–8

1 lb dried brown beans

5 cups water

8 ounces turkey tasso, cut into
½-inch pieces

2 cups chopped onion

1 teaspoon ground black
pepper

½ teaspoon ground dry
mustard

½ teaspoon paprika

2 teaspoons raw sugar

1 teaspoon ground cinnamon

1 tablespoon salt, or to taste

Rinse the beans and combine with the water in a large non-reactive saucepan. Cover and refrigerate 8 hours or over night. When you are ready to cook, bring the beans to a boil, turn off the heat, cover and let soak while you are preparing the other ingredients.

Place the tasso, onions, pepper, mustard, paprika, raw sugar and cinnamon in the crock. Add the beans and the soaking liquid and stir to mix. Cover and cook on high for 2½–3½ or low for 5–7 hours. Remove approximately 1 cup of the beans and mash well with a fork. Return the mashed beans to the slow cooker. Stir in the salt and cook for another 30 minutes on high or 1 hour on low.

• •

Chef's notes: *Seasoned the same as its pork progenitor, turkey tasso, contains considerable less saturated fat and sodium. Made of cured and smoked turkey thigh meat, it's a great seasoning meat for beans and other southern dishes.*

• •

WINE SUGGESTION: A big Australian Shiraz would work well with this.

Lentils with Eggplant

SERVES 6-8

- 3 tablespoons extra virgin olive oil
- 2 cups chopped onion
- 1 cup chopped bell pepper
- 2 cups eggplant, skin on, cut into 1-inch cubes
- 2 cups chicken stock, page 40, or 1—14 oz can chicken broth
- 3 cups water

- 1 lb brown lentils
- 2 tablespoons chopped garlic
- ½ teaspoon ground cumin
- ½ teaspoon salt, or to taste
- ¼ teaspoon ground black pepper
- ¼ teaspoon white pepper
- ⅛ teaspoon cayenne pepper, or to taste

Heat the oil in a large skillet set over a medium-high heat. Sauté the chopped onion and bell pepper for about 10 minutes or until soft. Transfer the contents of the skillet to the slow cooker. Stir in the remaining ingredients, cover and cook on high for 3 hours or low for 6 hours.

• • • • • • • • • • • • • •

WINE SUGGESTION: An Italian red or a red Burgundy.

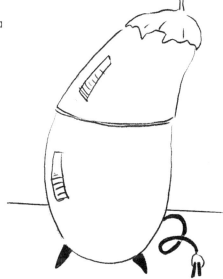

French Foreign Legion Lentils

SAME OLD LENTILS GOT YOU DOWN? Weary of plebeian preparations of prosaic pulses? Eliminate that epicurean ennui with these extramundane Gallic legumes. Varieties of lentils are legion in number, and firm, dark green French lentils cook up to a treat extraordinaire! This recipe employs an Algerian motif with hints of allspice, red pepper and cinnamon.

3 tablespoons extra virgin olive oil

2 cups finely chopped shallots

1 tablespoons minced garlic

1 teaspoon ground coriander

1 teaspoon ground cumin

½ teapsoon ground allspice

¼ teaspoon ground cinnamon

½ teaspoon ground black pepper

2 14½ ounce cans diced tomatoes, or 3½ cups diced fresh tomatoes

2 teaspoons Harissa hot sauce; or ¼ teaspoon Tabasco, or to taste

4½ cups chicken stock (page 40) or broth

1 lb French "Du Puy style" lentils

16 whole, peeled garlic cloves

¼ cup chopped parsley

½ teaspoon salt, or to taste

2 tablespoons fresh lemon juice

Heat the olive oil in a large skillet set over a high heat. Add the chopped shallots and sauté, stirring often, until lightly browned—about 6 to 8 minutes. Stir in the minced garlic, coriander, cumin, allspice, cinnamon and black pepper. Remove the pan from the heat and stir in the diced tomatoes with the liquid, if using canned, and the hot sauce.

Transfer the contents of the pan to the slow cooker, along with the stock, lentils and peeled garlic cloves. Stir to mix, cover and cook on low for 7–9 hours or high for 4–5 hours.

Stir in the chopped parsley, salt and lemon juice, adjust the seasoning, cover and cook for an additional 15–30 minutes.

Serve in large bowls over whole grain couscous, if desired.

• •

Chef's Notes: *If you must have meat, quickly brown a few links of lamb sausage, in a little olive oil and place them on top of the other ingredients at the beginning of the cooking.*

• •

WINE SUGGESTION: The centuries long cultural interchanges between North Africa and the Iberian peninsula would make a Spanish wine appropriate. Try a white Rueda or a red Rioja.

White Beans with Rosemary and Vermouth

SERVES 6–8

JOE'S A BIG FAN OF VERMOUTH, and not just for the six or eight drops he uses to soften the gin of his two martinis. As herb-infused wines, both sweet red and dry white add complexity and nuance to many a dish. Here, white vermouth mingled with the flavors of savory shallots and woodsy rosemary supplant the need for meat or stock.

1 **lb Great Northern White Beans**	2 **tablespoons minced fresh rosemary**
6 **cups water**	3 **bay leaves, crushed**
3 **tablespoons extra virgin olive oil, divided**	½ **teaspoon white pepper**
	⅛ **teaspoon cayenne pepper**
1 **cup finely chopped onions**	1 **cup white vermouth, divided**
1 **cup finely chopped shallots**	¼ **cup chopped parsley**
2 **tablespoons minced garlic**	1 **teaspoon salt, or to taste**

Rinse the beans and combine with the water in a large saucepan. Cover and refrigerate 8 hours or over night. When you are ready to cook, bring the beans to a boil, turn off the heat, cover and let soak while you are preparing the other ingredients.

Heat 2 tablespoons olive oil in a large skillet. Add the finely chopped onion and shallot and cook over a medium high heat for 6–8 minutes, stirring often until lightly browned. Stir in the minced garlic, rosemary, bay leaves, white pepper and cayenne pepper and cook for one more minute.

Transfer the content of the skillet to the slow cooker. Add the beans and the soaking liquid. Stir in ½ cup of the vermouth, cover and cook on low for 6–7 hours or high for 3–3½ hours. When the beans are tender, stir in the remaining tablespoon of olive oil, the remaining ½ cup of vermouth, the chopped parsley and salt to taste. Cook an additional 10–15 minutes.

Chef's Notes: *One of the benefits of cooking beans in a slow cooker really shows up here. The soft and delicate Great Northern White will retain their shape when cooked, rather get cooked down into a near purée.*

WINE SUGGESTION: A red or white Côtes du Rhône.

Red Beans with Smoked Turkey

SERVES 6–8

SMOKED TURKEY IS AN EASY REPLACEMENT for the ham hock or smoked pork sausage usually employed to season traditional Red Beans and Rice. Much lower in saturated fat and sodium, and higher in protein, the flavor complements and enhances red kidney beans.

- 1 lb dried dark red kidney beans
- 6 cups water
- 1 smoked turkey thigh, about 1 lb
- 1 tablespoon extra virgin olive oil
- 2 cups chopped onion
- 1½ cups chopped green bell pepper
- 1 cup chopped celery
- 1 tablespoon minced garlic
- 3 bay leaves, crushed
- 1 teaspoon dried whole thyme
- 1 teaspoon black pepper
- ⅛ teaspoon cayenne pepper, or to taste
- 1 tablespoon balsamic vinegar
- 1 teaspoon salt, or to taste
- 3 tablespoons chopped parsley

Rinse the beans and place them in a large, non-reactive saucepan, and pour in the water. Cover and refrigerate 8 hours or overnight.

Place the saucepan over a medium heat, bring it to a gentle boil, remove from the heat, cover and set aside while preparing the other ingredients,

Remove the skin and any visible fat from the smoked turkey thigh and place it in the crock. Heat the olive oil in large skillet set over a medium-high heat and add the chopped onion, bell pepper and celery. Sauté for 6–8 minutes or until softened. Stir in the garlic, bay leaf, thyme, black pepper and cayenne and cook for one minute. Transfer the contents of the pan to the crock, add the beans with the soaking liquid, cover and cook on high for 3–4 hours or low for 6–8 hours or until the beans are tender.

Remove the turkey thigh to a plate to cool. Remove about ¼ cup of the beans to a small bowl. Mash the beans with the back of a spoon until smooth and stir back into the crock along with the vinegar. Add salt to taste and stir in the parsley. When the turkey thigh is cool enough to handle, remove the meat from the bone, cut into bite-sized pieces, and stir them into the beans. Serve in large bowls, over steamed brown rice if desired.

• •

Chef's Notes: *When shopping for smoked turkey, look for an all-natural brand without added nitrites, available at natural food stores and many supermarkets (Diestel is a good brand), or smoke your own. Some grocery store "house smoked" varieties are over-cooked, too smoky and too salty.*

• •

WINE SUGGESTION: A fruity Pinot Noir or a full bodied Chardonnay.

Vegetarian Chili

THIS IS A PLEASER FOR A CROWD OF VEGETARIANS, and regular folk too. The lentils and grated zucchini give this chili a "meaty" body, and the green peppers, red beans, yellow corn and black beans—not to mention the garnishes—make it quite colorful.

1 cup dried pinto beans

1 cup dried dark red kidney beans

1 cup dried green lentils

7 cups water

2 tablespoons extra virgin olive oil

4 cups chopped onion

2 cups chopped poblano pepper or green bell pepper

1 large fresh jalapeño pepper, finely chopped (about 2 tablespoons), or to taste

¼ cup finely chopped garlic

1 tablespoon chipotle chili powder

3 tablespoons mild chili powder

1 tablespoon ground cumin

1 teaspoon dried whole oregano

1 6 ounce can tomato paste

1 medium-sized zucchini, shredded on a medium grater, about 2 cups

1½ cups corn kernels, fresh or frozen (optional)

1 teaspoon salt, or to taste

1 tablespoon fresh lime juice

1 14½ ounce can black beans, drained

GARNISHES (optional):

Thinly sliced green onion

Lime wedges

Chopped cilantro

Chopped fresh or pickled jalapeño peppers

Chopped fresh tomato

Crumbled queso fresca, or grated cheddar or jack cheese

Warm whole grain tortillas

Rinse the pinto beans, kidney beans and lentils and place them in a large, non-reactive saucepan along with the water. Cover and refrigerate 8 hours or overnight. When ready to cook, place the saucepan over a medium heat, bring it to a gentle boil, remove from the heat, cover and let set while preparing the other ingredients.

Heat the olive oil in a large skillet set over a medium-high heat. Add the chopped onion, poblano or green bell pepper and finely chopped jalapeño. Cook, stirring occasionally, for 8–10 minutes, or until onions are softened. Add the garlic, chili powders, cumin and oregano and stir to mix. Stir in the tomato paste and cook, stirring often, for 2–3 minutes. Transfer the contents of the pan to the crock, along with the beans and their soaking liquid, the zucchini and corn (if using). Cover and cook on high for 3–4 hours or low for 6–8 hours, or until beans are tender.

Stir in the salt, lime juice and drained black beans and continue cooking on high for ½ hour or low for 1 hour.

Serve in large bowls with garnishes as desired.

• •

Chef's Notes: *Canned black beans are added at the end because soaking dried black beans with the others tend to discolor them.*

• •

WINE SUGGESTION: There are so many flavors here that a lot of things would work. Try an Argentine Malbec, California Zinfandel, a red Côtes du Rhône or a full-bodied Chardonnay. Homemade sangria or Mexican beer would also be a good choice.

Dal

*I*N INDIA, DAL IS THE GENERIC TERM for dried beans and peas, and the dishes prepared with them. Enlightened to the world of dal while sitting at the foot of the master at an ashram in Rishikesh, Joe offers this basic, yet absolutely delicious recipe. There are infinite variations, and with practice, an entire universe of recipe possibilities will unfold (consider the number of mustard seeds in 2 tablespoons)—but they are all, in essence, simply dal.

1 lb yellow split peas	2 cups chopped onion
5 cups water	1 tablespoon minced garlic
2 teaspoons powdered turmeric	2 tablespoons minced fresh ginger
2 teaspoons ground cumin	1 tablespoon minced fresh
1 teaspoon ground coriander	jalapeño pepper, or to
¼ teaspoon cayenne pepper, or to taste	taste
2 tablespoons canola oil	2 cups chopped fresh tomato, or 1-14½ ounce can
2 tablespoons black mustard seed	"petite cut" diced tomato
2 tablespoons whole cumin seeds	1 teaspoon salt, or to taste
	Raw or dry roasted cashew nut for garnish (optional)

Combine the yellow split peas, water, turmeric, ground cumin, ground coriander and cayenne pepper in the crock. Stir, cover and cook on high for 3½–4½ hours or low for 7–9 hours, or until peas are tender and begin to break apart.

Heat the oil in a large skillet set over a medium-high heat. Add the black mustard seeds and cumin seeds and cook for 1 or 2 minutes, until the mustard seeds start to pop and sputter and turn gray. Stir in the chopped onion, minced garlic, ginger and jalapeño and cook, stirring often, for 6–8 minutes or until the onions are soft. Transfer the contents of the pan to the crock and stir in the chopped or diced tomato and salt. Cover and continue cooking on high for ½ hour or low for 1 hour.

Serve over steamed brown basmati rice and garnish with cashew nuts, if desired.

● ●

Chef's Notes: *What is the meaning of life?*

● ●

WINE SUGGESTION: What would Siddhartha drink? The wise may enjoy a simple glass of water, or perhaps ice water, or a cup of tea. Others may appreciate an Austrian Gruner Veltliner, a California Gewürztraminer, an Alsace Riesling, or anything German. If you're in a colonial mood, have a British-brewed India Pale Ale, or in a nod to the sub-continent, try a Kingfisher lager. After all, it's all relative, apparently.

Brown Rice

THE HEALTH-GIVING PROPERTIES of brown rice are almost mythic, and its culinary applications are global. Be sure to read "About Slow Cooker Rice" on the next page before preparing these recipes.

Basic Brown Rice
Mexican Rice with Black Beans and Corn
Curried Rice with Cauliflower, Carrots and Peas
Rice Pilaf with Arugula and Walnuts
Caribbean Rice and Peas
Arroz sin Pollo
Arroz con Quimbombó
Asian Rice with Carrots, Spinach and Almonds
Wild Mushroom Pilaf

*Nutritional analysis available at
www.joesimmer.com,
courtesy of Corey C. Walsh, LDN, RD*

61

About Slow Cooker
Brown Rice

RICE IN A SLOW COOKER CAN BE A CHALLENGE, but by following a few simple rules, delicious, nutritious rice dishes are a snap. Because of the lower heat, rice takes longer to cook in a slow cooker, and because there is less evaporation, it requires less liquid than stove-top steamed rice.

Use short grain brown rice. This variety doesn't get starchy or too sticky like some other varieties do, and it has a wonderful, risotto-like texture.

Always get all the other ingredients up to a boil before adding them to the crock and stirring in the brown rice. Otherwise, it will take too long for the whole volume of ingredients to reach a simmer, causing the rice around the edges of the crock to cook much sooner than the rice in the center.

Always cook your short grain brown rice on the "high" setting.

In general, after a cooking time of 2 hours on high, the rice is gently tossed with two forks to mix and fluff, and then cooked or left to rest for and additional 30 minutes. Each recipe has complete instructions.

The recipes in this book were tested in a 6-quart oval slow cooker. These brown rice recipes may take longer to cook in round or other size cookers, resulting in some of the rice being over cooked. Joe has found the widely available 6-quart oval, programmable model to be the most versatile and convenient slow cooker.

Basic Brown Rice

MAKES 5 CUPS COOKED RICE

3½ cups water
2 cups short grain brown rice, rinsed

½ teaspoon salt, or to taste
1 teaspoon extra virgin olive oil

Read about slow cooker brown rice (page 62). In a small saucepan, bring the water to a boil, then transfer it to the crock along with the other ingredients. Stir, cover and cook on high for 2 hours.

Using two forks, gently toss the rice in the crock to mix and fluff. Cover and let rest on the "keep warm" setting for 10–30 minutes before serving.

• •

Chef's Notes: *If you are saving some of the rice for later use, remove it to another container to cool after the resting period.*

• •

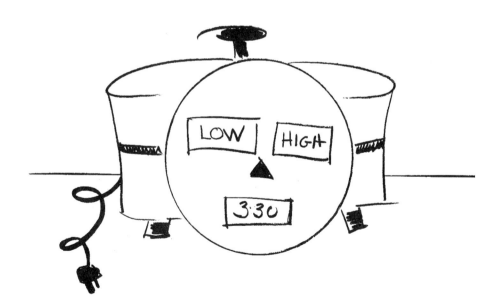

Mexican Rice
with Black Beans and Corn

SERVES 6–8

2 tablespoons extra virgin
  olive oil

2 cups chopped white onion

1 cup chopped green bell
  pepper

1 tablespoon minced Jalapeno
  pepper, seeds removed
  before chopping

2 tablespoons mild chili
  powder

½ teaspoon salt, or to taste

3 cups chicken stock (page 40)
  or low-sodium broth

1 14½ ounce can petite diced
  tomatoes

2 cups short grain brown rice,
  rinsed

1½ cups frozen corn, thawed

1 14¼ ounce can black beans,
  drained

¼ cup chopped cilantro

Read about slow cooker brown rice (page 62). Heat the olive oil in a large skillet set over a medium-high heat. Add the chopped onion, bell pepper and Jalapeno and cook, stirring occasionally for 8–10 minutes. Stir in the chili powder and salt and cook for 1 minute. Add the chicken stock and diced tomatoes, with liquid, to the pan and bring to a boil, stirring often. Transfer the contents of the pan to the crock and stir in the short grain brown rice. Cover and cook on high for 2 hours.

Add the thawed corn, drained black beans and chopped cilantro, and using two forks, gently toss to mix and fluff. Adjust the seasoning, cover and continue cooking on high for about 30 minutes, or until rice is done.

• •

WINE SUGGESTION: A Chilean Sauvignon Blanc, an Argentine Malbec, or a Mexican beer.

Curried Rice
with Cauliflower, Carrots
and Peas

SERVES 6–8

1 tablespoon canola oil

2 cups chopped onion

3 cups bite-sized cauliflower
  flowerets

1 cup ¼-inch thick sliced
  carrots

2 tablespoons curry powder

1 teaspoon salt, or to taste

1½ cups chicken stock (page 40)
  or broth, or vegetable
  stock (page 39) or broth

1 14 ounce can coconut milk
  or "lite" coconut milk

2 cups short grain brown rice,
  rinsed

1½ cups frozen green peas,
  thawed

½ cup raw or dry roasted
  cashew nuts, coarsely
  chopped (optional)

Read about slow cooker brown rice (page 62). Heat the oil in a large skillet set over a medium-high heat. Add the chopped onion and sauté for 5–6 minutes, stirring occasionally, until softened and lightly browned. Stir in the cauliflower and carrots and cook for 1 minute. Add the curry powder and salt, stir to mix, then add the chicken stock or broth and bring to a boil. Transfer the contents of the pan to the crock and stir in the coconut milk and brown rice. Cover and cook on high for 2 hours.

Add the thawed peas to the crock and, using two forks, gently toss to mix them in. Cover and continue cooking on high for an additional 30 minutes, or until rice is done. Garnish with cashew nuts if desired.

• •

WINE SUGGESTION: A Vouvray from France's Loire valley, in any of its many incarnations, would work well, as would an Alsace or German Riesling, Gewurztraminer or Müller-Thurgau, in any of their many incarnations.

Rice Pilaf
with Arugula and Walnuts

SERVES 6–8

ONCE WHILE WOOING A GIRL FROM PARIS, Joe found himself running up against a brick wall of resistance. A vegetarian and part-time chanteuse at the neighborhood jazz club, the raven-haired Marie always rebuffed Joe's sincere advances. C'est dommage, mais, c'est la vie.

For his final attempt at storming the Bastille of her heart, one sultry mid-July evening Joe prepared a romantic dinner of this brown rice pilaf, a nice endive salad with heirloom tomatoes and Roquefort cheese vinaigrette, and a bottle of the best Burgundy he could afford. With such a flawlessly executed healthy meal, the evening was a coup, and the rest is history.

- 2 tablespoons extra virgin olive oil
- 1½ cups finely chopped shallot
- 1 teaspoon black pepper
- ½ teaspoon salt, or to taste
- 3 cups chicken stock (page 40), or broth
- ½ cup dry white wine
- 2 cups short grain brown rice
- 5 ounces baby arugula, stems removed, about 6 cups
- ½ cup coarsely chopped walnuts

Read about slow cooker brown rice (page 62). Heat the olive oil in a large skillet set over a medium-high heat. Add the chopped shallot and sauté, stirring often for 5–6 minutes. Stir in the black pepper, salt, chicken stock and wine. Bring the mixture to a boil, stirring occasionally. Transfer the contents of the pan to the crock and stir in the short grain brown rice. Cover and cook on high for 2 hours. Gently fold in the arugula and walnuts, cover, lower heat to "keep warm" and let set for 10–15 minutes or until rice is done. Using two forks, gently toss to mix and fluff before serving.

Chefs Notes: *Arugula is delicious, but if you don't like it or can't find it, substitute an equal amount of baby spinach.*

WINE SUGGESTION: A white Burgundy, or an un-oaked Chardonnay from France, California or Australia.

"Je ne marque de rien"

Caribbean Rice and Peas

SERVES 6-8

VARIATIONS OF THIS DISH are found all over the Caribbean, and it is quite popular in Jamaica, where all beans are referred to as peas. Traditionally cow peas or field peas are used, but red kidney beans, black beans and others are also common.

1 tablespoon extra virgin olive oil

2 cups chopped onion

1 tablespoon minced garlic

½ teaspoon black pepper

⅛ teaspoon cayenne pepper, or to taste

½ teaspoon salt, or to taste

1 bay leaf, crushed

1¾ cups chicken stock (page 39), or low-sodium broth

1 14 ounce can field peas, black-eyed peas or other beans, drained

1 14 ounce can coconut milk or "lite" coconut milk

2 cups short grain brown rice, rinsed

3 tablespoons chopped parsley

1 tablespoon fresh lemon juice

Read about slow cooker brown rice (page 62). Heat the olive oil in a medium sized skillet set over a medium-high heat. Add the chopped onion and sauté for 5–6 minutes until softened. Stir in the garlic, black pepper, cayenne, salt and bay leaf and cook for an additional minute. Add the chicken stock and drained peas to the skillet and bring to a boil, stirring often. Meanwhile, place the coconut milk and rinsed rice in the crock. When the onion/stock mixture is at a good boil, transfer to the crock and stir to mix. Cover and cook on high for 2 hours.

Sprinkle in the parsley and lemon juice, and using 2 forks, gently toss to mix. Cover and continue cooking on high for an additional 30 minutes or until rice is done. Gently toss once more, adjust seasoning, cover and let set on "keep warm" until ready to serve.

WINE SUGGESTION: Forgo the wine and enjoy a ginger beer or a Red Stripe.

Arroz sin Pollo

SERVES 6–8

ARROZ <u>CON</u> POLLO is found all over Latin America, and it seems to be culinary kin to both paella and jambalaya. The seasonings and vegetable content vary from region to region, but Joe took the variation in a bold new direction by eliminating the chicken. Thus, Arroz <u>sin</u> Pollo—it's the same, only different.

1 tablespoon extra virgin olive oil

2 cups chopped onion

1 cup chopped green bell pepper

3 tablespoons minced garlic

1 teaspoon ground cumin

½ teaspoon black pepper

¼ teaspoon cayenne pepper, or to taste

½ teaspoon salt

3 cups chicken stock (page 40) or broth

1 14½ ounce can diced tomatoes, un-drained

1 14½ ounce can quartered artichoke hearts, drained and rinsed (optional)

2 cups short grain brown rice, rinsed

¼ teaspoon saffron threads

1 tablespoon warm water

1 cup frozen green peas, thawed

¾ cups pimento stuffed green olives, drained and coarsely chopped

1 tablespoon fresh lime juice, or more to taste

Read about slow cooker brown rice (page 62). Heat the olive oil in a large skillet set over a medium-high heat. Add the chopped onion and bell pepper and sauté for 8–10 minutes, stirring occasionally, until softened and lightly browned. Stir in the garlic, cumin, black pepper, cayenne pepper and salt and cook for 1 minute. Add the chicken stock or broth and un-drained diced tomatoes to the skillet and bring to a boil. Transfer the contents of the pan to the crock and stir in the artichoke hearts and brown rice. Cover and cook on high for 2 hours.

Combine the saffron threads and warm water in a small bowl and allow it to soak while rice is cooking. Add the saffron and water to the crock along with the thawed peas and coarsely chopped olives and, using two forks, gently toss to mix them in. Cover and continue cooking on high for an additional 30 minutes, or until rice is done.

Sprinkle in the fresh lime juice, toss again with two forks, cover and let set for 5–10 minutes before serving.

• •

Chef's Notes: *For Arroz <u>con</u> Pollo, add 1½ lbs of cooked boneless, skinless chicken at the time you add the peas and olives.*

• •

WINE SUGGESTION: Try a light-bodied Tempranillo for red or an Albariño for white—both Spanish.

Arroz con Quimbombó

SERVES 6–8

ALTHOUGH NOT WELL KNOWN IN THE FAMILY, Joe's father's cousin Giacomo Simoni did a little clandestine work for the CIA way back when—some kind of mutually beneficial deal he made with the feds around the time he left New Jersey. While on covert assignment in Cuba, he stumbled upon this dish at an obscure downtown Havana Afro-Cuban music hall, which served as a front for a secret U.S. government backed cigar factory.

- 2 tablespoons extra virgin olive oil
- 2 cups chopped onion
- 1 cup chopped green bell pepper
- 1 tablespoon minced garlic
- 1 teaspoon salt, or to taste
- ½ teaspoon black pepper
- ⅛ teaspoon cayenne pepper, or to taste
- 1 cup tomato sauce
- 1 tablespoon white wine vinegar
- 1 lb sliced okra, fresh or frozen
- ¾ lb turkey "chorizo" or other turkey sausage or chicken sausage
- 2 cups chicken stock
- ½ cup dry white wine
- 2 cups short grain brown rice

Read about slow cooker brown rice (page 62). Heat the olive oil in a large skillet set over a medium-high heat and cook the chopped onion and bell pepper, stirring occasionally, until softened and a slightly browned. Stir in the minced garlic, salt, black pepper and cayenne pepper and cook for 2 more minutes. Add the tomato sauce, vinegar, okra, sausage, chicken stock, and wine to the pan and bring to a boil, stirring often. Transfer the contents of the pan to the crock and stir in the brown rice. Cover and cook on high for 2 hours.

Using two forks, toss to mix, adjust the seasoning and continue cooking on high for an additional 30 minutes, or until rice is done.

● ●

Chef's Notes: *"Quimbombó" is the Cuban word for okra, very similar to the African "kingombo", which is considered the origin of the word "gumbo". This dish has a similar flavor profile to many New Orleans gumbos, but the rice is cooked in it, as seen in some Spanish dishes such as paella, and similar to jambalaya.*

● ●

WINE SUGGESTION: Try a Tempranillo if you are interested in something red. If not, a full bodied Chardonnay would be muy bueno.

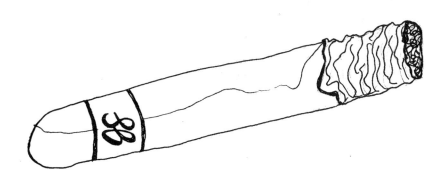

Asian Rice with Carrots, Spinach and Almonds

SERVES 6–8

A HEALTHY ALTERNATIVE TO FRIED RICE.

1 tablespoon canola oil

2 cups chopped onion

2 cups carrots, diagonally sliced, ¼ inch thick

1 tablespoon minced garlic

1 tablespoon minced or grated fresh ginger

⅛ teaspoon cayenne pepper, or to taste

1 teaspoon toasted sesame oil

3¼ cups chicken stock (page 40) or broth

3 tablespoons low sodium soy sauce

2 cups short grain brown rice, rinsed

5 ounces fresh baby spinach, stems removed, about 6 cups

½ cup raw or dry roasted almonds, coarsely chopped

½ cups chopped cilantro

Read about slow cooker brown rice (page 62). In a large skillet set over a medium-high heat, sauté the onions and carrots in the oil for 6–8 minutes, stirring often, until they begin to brown. Stir in the garlic, ginger, cayenne pepper and sesame oil and cook for 1 minute. Add the chicken stock and soy sauce and bring the mixture to a boil, stirring often. Transfer the contents of the pan to the crock and stir in the short grain brown rice, cover and cook on high for 2 hours or until rice is done.

Add the spinach, almonds and cilantro, and using two forks gently toss to mix and fluff. Cover and let rest on "keep warm" for 10–15 minutes. Then gently toss once more before serving.

···

Chef's Notes: *For a variation, toss in 2 cups lightly steamed broccoli flowerets instead of or in addition to the spinach, and/or substitute raw or dry roasted cashew nuts for the almonds.*

···

WINE SUGGESTION: German wines tend to work well with Asian flavors, and any good quality Riesling or Gewürztraminer would be nice. If you want something dryer, try a Riesling from right across the border in Alsace.

Wild Mushroom Pilaf

SERVES 6–8

THE RICH, WOODSY FLAVORS OF THIS PILAF, served with a salad of seasonal greens would make a delicious and healthy light meal on a chilly autumn evening, or a welcomed new side dish for your Thanksgiving feast.

- ½ **ounce dried porcini mushrooms**
- 1 **cup boiling water**
- 2 **tablespoons extra virgin olive oil**
- 2 **cups finely chopped shallot**
- 1 **bay leaf, crushed**
- 1 **tablespoon chopped fresh rosemary**
- ½ **teaspoon dried thyme**
- 1 **teaspoon black pepper, or to taste**
- ⅛ **teaspoon cayenne pepper, or to taste**
- 1 **teaspoon salt, or to taste**
- 6 **ounces sliced baby Portobello mushrooms**
- 2½ **cups chicken stock (page 40) or low-sodium chicken broth**
- ½ **cup dry white wine**
- 2 **cups short grain brown rice, rinsed**
- ½ **cup chopped parsley**

Read about slow cooker brown rice (page 62). Place the dried porcinis in a small bowl and pour on the boiling water. Cover and soak for 30 minutes while preparing the other ingredients. Remove the porcinis from the soaking liquid, rinse them and finely chop. Strain the soaking liquid through a coffee filter or a piece of cheesecloth and reserve ½ cup.

Heat the oil in a large skillet set over a medium-high heat. Add the shallot and sauté, stirring occasionally, for 5–6 minutes, or until lightly browned. Add the bay leaf, rosemary, thyme, black pepper, cayenne pepper, salt, sliced baby Portobello mushrooms and finely chopped porcini mushrooms and cook for 3 minutes, stirring occasionally. Add the chicken stock or broth, white wine and the reserved ½ cup of porcini soaking liquid. Bring to a boil, stirring occasionally, and transfer the contents of the pan to the crock. Stir in the short grain brown rice, cover and cook on high for 2 hours or until rice is done.

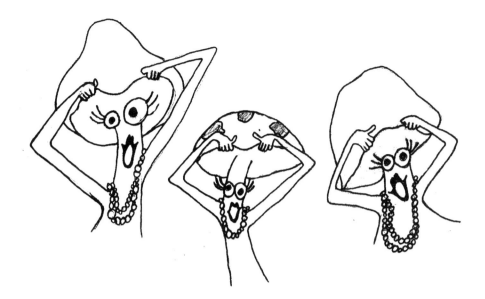

Add the chopped parsley, and using two forks, gently toss to mix and fluff before serving.

● ●

Chef's Notes: *For a more substantial dish, toss in a can of drained, rinsed chick peas and/or ½ cup of pine nuts when you add the parsley.*

● ●

WINE SUGGESTION: An earthy Pinot Noir or a full bodied Chardonnay.

Vegetable Entrées and Sides

WHENEVER JOE GETS ON A SERIOUS HEALTH BINGE or wants to shed a few pounds to get down to his fightin' weight, he embraces the vegetable entrée theory of health and slimness. Simply substitute a big plate of vegetables for your usual steak and potatoes, fried chicken and biscuits or double-cut pork chop with a side of macaroni and cheese. It's a great way fill up on a satisfying, low calorie, high fiber, nutritious meal, and as an added benefit, you don't feel tired or sluggish as you sometimes may after a higher density dinner.

Curried Vegetable Stew
Ratatouille
Eggplant Bolognese
Posole Gumbo
Greek Green Beans in Tomato Sauce
Leeks and Mushrooms Provencal
Sweet Potato and Peanut Stew

Nutritional analysis available at
www.joesimmer.com,
courtesy of Corey C. Walsh, LDN, RD

79

Curried Vegetable Stew

SERVES 6

THIS RECIPE CALLS FOR MADRAS STYLE CURRY POWDER, typical of South Indian vegetarian cuisine. Available at Asian markets or on-line, it's a bit spicier than the standard grocery store variety. If you're not a fan of cayenne, or can't find Madras powder, use the readily available milder blend.

1 **tablespoon canola oil**	1 **small head cauliflower,**
1 **cup chopped onion**	**broken into flowerets**
1 **tablespoon minced ginger**	½ **pound carrots, scrubbed and**
2 **tablespoon Madras style**	**cut into ½ inch slices**
or other curry powder	½ **pound fresh green beans,**
½ **teaspoon salt, or to taste**	**trimmed and broken in**
2 **14 ounce cans "lite" coconut**	**half**
milk	½ **cup chopped fresh cilantro**
¾ **cup red lentils, rinsed**	2 **tablespoons fresh lime juice**

Heat the oil in a medium-sized skillet set over a medium-high heat. Add the chopped onion and cook, stirring occasionally, for 4–5 minutes or until softened. Remove the pan from the heat and stir in the grated ginger, curry powder and salt. Set aside.

Pour 1 can of the coconut milk into the crock, and stir in the red lentils. Add the cauliflower, carrots and green beans. Pour the remaining can of coconut milk into the skillet of sautéed onions, ginger and curry powder. Stir well to deglaze, and then pour the contents of the pan over the vegetables in the crock. Do not stir at this point. Cover and cook on high for 3–4 hours or low for 6–8 hours. If possible, stir once about halfway through.

Adjust the seasoning, stir in the cilantro and lime juice and serve as is or over steamed brown basmati rice.

· ·

Chef's Notes: *Be sure to use red lentils, available at most natural food stores or on-line. Red lentils cook quickly and completely disintegrate, serving as a thickening agent for the gravy. They also have a great flavor. Substituting other varieties will not work with this recipe.*

· ·

WINE SUGGESTION: A dry Alsace Riesling or an Austrian Gruner Veltliner would be like nirvana with this dish.

Ratatouille

1 large eggplant, about 1¼-1½ lbs, cut into ¾ inch cubes
Salt
2 tablespoons extra virgin olive oil
3 cups chopped onion
2 tablespoons chopped garlic
1 tablespoon minced fresh rosemary
1 teaspoon dried whole thyme
1 teaspoon dried whole oregano
½ teaspoon black pepper
2 14½ ounce cans diced tomatoes, drained
1 large zucchini, about ½ lb, cut in half lengthwise and sliced into ½ inch half-circles
1 large yellow squash, about ½ lb, cut in half length-wise and sliced into ½ inch half-circles
¼ cup chopped fresh basil

Place the eggplant cubes in a colander set in the sink and sprinkle liberally with salt. Toss to evenly distribute the salt and let it set for 30 minutes. Rinse the cubes, drain and pat dry.

Heat the oil in a large non-stick skillet over a medium-high heat. Add the chopped onion and cook, stirring occasionally, for 6–8 minutes. Add the garlic, rosemary, thyme, oregano and black pepper and cook for 1 minute. Add the eggplant cubes and cook for 3–4 minutes, stirring often. Transfer the contents of the pan to the crock. Add the drained diced tomatoes, sliced zucchini and sliced yellow squash. Stir to mix, cover and cook for 2–3 hours on high or 4–6 hours on low, or until the eggplant is tender.

Adjust the seasoning and stir in the chopped fresh basil.

• •

Chef's Notes: *Salting the eggplant will remove any bitterness and some of the excess moisture. Usually there is enough residual salt that you won't have to add any more.*

• •

WINE SUGGESTION: A nice Chianti or a Cotes du Rhone.

Eggplant Bolognese

SERVES 6-8

MANY THINK A TOMATO SAUCE must include meat to be termed "Bolognese", but Joe considers that a lotta baloney. When Joe's friend Boudreaux was touring Italy, he met a old vegetarian in Bologna, Vitale DiFatta, who gave him this meat-free recipe.

6 cups eggplant, cut into ¼ inch cubes

2 cups zucchini, cut into ¼ inch cubes

1 tablespoon salt

3 tablespoons extra virgin olive oil

2 cups chopped onion

1 tablespoon chopped garlic

½ cup red wine

2 6 ounce cans tomato paste

1 teaspoon ground black pepper

2 tablespoons fresh oregano leaves

½ cup chicken stock (page 40) or broth

Parmesan cheese, grated (optional)

Place the eggplant and zucchini cubes in a colander, sprinkle them with salt, place the colander in the sink or over bowl and allow to "weep" for ½ hour.

Heat the olive oil in a large, non-stick skillet or frying pan set over a medium-high heat and sauté the eggplant, zucchini, chopped onion and garlic for 10 minutes, stirring frequently. If your pan isn't large enough to hold everything, use two pans, or sauté in batches. Transfer the contents of the skillet to the slow cooker.

Deglaze the skillet with the wine until reduced by one half, scraping the bottom well. Transfer to slow cooker. Stir in the tomato paste, pepper, oregano leaves and chicken stock and mix well. Cover and cook on low for 6 hours.

Stir the contents of the slow cooker, scraping sides well. Serve over your favorite whole grain pasta. Sprinkle with freshly grated Parmesan cheese if desired.

Chef's Notes: *Chilled or at room temperature, this makes a great hors d'oeuvres spread on whole-wheat crackers or toast points.*

WINE SUGGESTION: Anything Italian, white or red.

Posole Gumbo

CALLED HOMINY IN THE SOUTH, posole is a staple in some areas of Mexico and the American Southwest. This is a delicious South/Southwest fusion dish.

12 ounces dried posole

3 cups water

2 tablespoons extra virgin olive oil

3 cups chopped onion

1 cup chopped celery

1 cup chopped green bell pepper

1 tablespoon minced garlic

1 tablespoon minced jalapeno pepper, seeds removed before mincing

1 teaspoon black pepper

½ teaspoon white pepper

½ teaspoon cayenne pepper, or to taste

½ teaspoon dried whole thyme

½ teaspoon salt, or to taste

3 bay leaves, crushed

1 lb sliced okra, fresh or frozen

1 tablespoon balsamic vinegar

2 14½ ounce can diced tomato

6 cups chicken stock (page 40) or broth; or vegetable stock (page 39) or broth

¼ cup chopped parsley

Place the dried posole and water in a non-reactive saucepan and refrigerate over night. When you are ready to cook, bring the pan to a boil, remove it from the heat and let set while preparing the other ingredients.

Heat the olive oil in a large skillet set over a medium high heat. Add the chopped onion, celery and bell pepper and cook, stirring occasionally, for 10–12 minutes until softened and lightly browned. Stir in the minced garlic, minced jalapeno, black pepper, white pepper, cayenne pepper, thyme, salt and bay leaves and cook for another 2–3 minutes.

Place the sliced okra in the crock and sprinkle on the balsamic vinegar. Add the diced tomatoes, including the liquid, and scrape in the contents of the skillet. Pour in the chicken or vegetable stock and the posole and its soaking liquid. Stir to mix, cover and cook on high for 3½–4½ hours or low for 7–9 hours, or until the posole is tender. Adjust the seasoning and stir in the chopped parsley.

Serve in large bowls over steamed brown basmati rice.

• •

WINE SUGGESTION: A crisp Sauvignon Blanc.

Greek Green Beans in Tomato Sauce

JOE'S COUSIN MELBA WAS A PRETTY GIRL, but never did too much in the way of making the most of her natural attributes. Her hair was a mess, her clothes ill fitting and out of style, and her posture atrocious. Though only slightly over weight, she lacked any muscle tone, and there was no glow to her complexion and no gleam in her eye. Usually lost in her thoughts, she seemed blissfully unaware of her looks, until one day, while checking her balance at an ATM machine, she glanced up at the security mirror. Its cruel convex reflection revealed a group of callous sophisticates mocking her homely demeanor.

Stung by this brutal humiliation, Melba shuffled home, where waiting in the day's mail was cousin Joe's new Healthy Slow Cookin' book. She dusted off her crock, pulled some old gym clothes out of her college-days foot locker, and went to work. With wild determination, and Joe's help, she vowed never to be mocked again!

Here's one of her favorite life changing recipes.

1½ **lbs fresh green beans, trimmed**
1 **6 oz can tomato paste**
1 **tablespoon chopped garlic**
1½ **cups chicken stock (page 40) or low-sodium broth**
½ **teaspoon salt, or to taste**
½ **teaspoon ground black pepper**
Pinch of cayenne pepper (optional)
¼ **cup chopped pitted Kalamata olives (optional)**
1 **tablespoon chopped fresh parsley or basil (optional)**

Place the green beans, tomato paste, garlic, chicken stock, salt and peppers in the slow cooker and stir to mix—scraping any tomato paste that sticks to the sides back into the mixture. Cover and cook on high for 3–4 hours, or until beans are tender. Stir in the chopped olives and fresh parsley or basil, if using, and cook for an additional 15–30 minutes. Stir once more, again scraping sides of cooker, before serving.

• •

Chef's Notes: *For a slight variation, add one medium onion, cut in half and sliced into thin slices along with the beans, tomato paste, etc., and reduce the chicken stock to 1 cup. For a vegan version of this dish, use vegetable stock instead of chicken stock.*

• •

Leeks and Mushrooms Provencal

SERVES 6-8

2 tablespoons extra virgin olive oil

2 bunches leeks, white part cleaned and chopped into ½-inch rings, about 2 cups

1 cup chopped onions

1 tablespoon minced garlic

¼ cup white wine

1 teaspoon salt

½ teaspoon ground black pepper

1 14½ ounce can diced tomatoes, drained

½ teaspoon Dijon mustard

8 ounces sliced baby portabella mushrooms

2 anchovy filets, mashed

10 jumbo pitted black olives, sliced into ⅛ inch rings

1 tablespoon lemon juice

Heat the oil in a medium skillet over a medium heat. Sauté the leeks, onions and garlic for about 8–10 minutes until soft. Transfer contents of skillet to slow cooker. Deglaze the skillet with the wine and transfer to the slow cooker.

Add salt, pepper, drained tomatoes and mustard to the slow cooker. Stir together. Cook on high for 2½ hours.

Add mushrooms, anchovies, olives and lemon juice. Cook for another 1 hour on high.

● ●

WINE SUGGESTION: A Côtes du Rhône, red or white, or a fruity Beaujolais.

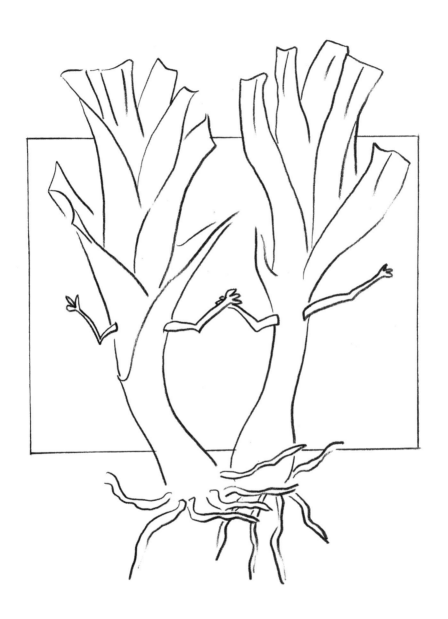

Sweet Potato and Peanut Stew

SERVES 6-8

2 tablespoons extra virgin olive oil

3 cups chopped onion

1 cup chopped green bell pepper

1 tablespoon minced jalapeño pepper, or to taste

2 tablespoons minced garlic

2 tablespoons minced ginger root

2 tablespoons mild chili powder

1 tablespoon ground cumin

¼ teaspoon cayenne pepper, or to taste

1 teaspoon salt, or to taste

½ cup tomato paste

3 large sweet potatoes (about 3 lbs) peeled and cut into 1 inch dice

1½ cups vegetable stock

¾ cup natural peanut butter, smooth or chunky

½ cup thinly sliced green onion

¼ cup chopped parsley

Coarsely chopped dry-roasted peanuts (optional)

Heat the olive oil in a large skillet set over a medium heat. Add the onion, bell pepper and jalapeño pepper and sauté, stirring occasionally for 10–12 minutes. Stir in the minced garlic, minced ginger, chili powder, cumin, cayenne pepper and salt and cook, stirring often, for 3 minutes. Remove the pan from the heat and stir in the tomato paste until evenly mixed. Transfer the contents of the pan to the crock, along with the diced sweet potatoes and vegetable stock. Cover and cook on high for 2– 3 hours or on low for 4–6 hours, or until sweet potatoes are tender, yet firm.

Scoop out about 1 cup of the liquid from the crock and mix it with the peanut butter until evenly blended. If necessary, add additional stock or hot water. Gently stir into the sweet potatoes, along with the green onions and parsley. Cover and cook on high for 30 minutes or low for 1 hour.

Serve over whole wheat couscous, if desired, and garnish with chopped peanuts, if desired.

• •

Chef's Notes: *Some varieties of sweet potatoes cook faster than others, so be sure to check the crock at the low end of the cooking range. If by chance you do over-cook, you can whip these potatoes up into a nice mashed sweet potato dish.*

• •

WINE SUGGESTION: Ein, zwei, drei, vier—how many times has Joe recommended German wines for his spicy and/or exotically flavored dishes? Apparently not enough. A dry or off-dry Riesling or Gewürztraminer would do this dish proud.

Seafood Entrées

HIGH IN PROTEIN, low in fat, the benefits of omega-3 fatty acids—it's no news that seafood is good for you. What may be news is that you can use your slow cooker for many delicious seafood dishes. The key is adding the seafood at the end of the cooking process, and being careful not to let it over cook.

Thai Fish Stew
Redfish Courtbullion
Bouillabaisse
Curried Shrimp
Shrimp in Orange Sauce
Seafood Okra Gumbo
Poached Salmon with Dilled Dijon Sauce
Creole Stewed Shrimp
Red Snapper Veracruz

Nutritional analysis available at
www.joesimmer.com,
courtesy of Corey C. Walsh, LDN, RD

Thai Fish Stew

SERVES 6-8

OTHER THAN A BIT OF SLICING and chopping up front, this dish is amazingly easy to prepare—and very impressive!

5 cups thinly sliced shallots, cut into half-circles

2 cups ½-inch sliced carrots

2 jalapeno peppers, seeded and chopped, or to taste

⅓ cup finely chopped ginger

1 teaspoon grated lime rind

2 tablespoons fresh lime juice

2 14 ounce cans coconut milk, or 2—14 ounce can "lite" coconut milk, or one of each

¼ cup Thai fish sauce

4 stalks lemon grass, bruised

2 bay leaves, crushed

3 tablespoons curry powder

½ teaspoon black pepper

1 teaspoon salt

1 tablespoon raw sugar

½ cup thinly sliced fresh basil

1 cup chopped fresh cilantro, divided

1 5½ ounce can bamboo shoots, drained

2 lbs firm white fish such as mahi mahi, snapper, halibut, amberjack or grouper, cut into bite sized pieces

Combine the first 15 ingredients in the crock. Add ¾ cup of the chopped cilantro, stir to mix, cover and cook on high for 2–3 hours or low for 4–6 hours, or until vegetables are tender.

Stir in the bamboo shoots and fish and cook for an additional 15–30 minutes until fish is cooked through. Adjust the seasoning and remove the lemon grass and bay leaves. Serve in large soup plates, over steamed brown jasmine rice if desired, and garnish with the remaining cilantro.

• •

WINE SUGGESTION: As with many Asian dishes, an Austrian Gruner Veltliner or a dry California or Alsace Riesling.

Redfish Courtbouillon

SERVES 6–8

⅓ cup extra virgin olive oil

½ cup whole wheat pastry flour

1½ cups chopped onion

1 cup chopped green onion tops

½ cup chopped green bell pepper

1 tablespoon minced garlic

⅓ cup chopped celery

1 14½ ounce can diced tomatoes, including liquid

1 tablespoon chopped parsley

3 bay leaves, crushed

1 6 oz can tomato paste

½ teaspoon dried whole thyme

¼ teaspoon dried whole marjoram

½ teaspoon ground allspice

1 teaspoon salt

½ teaspoon black pepper

¼ teaspoon cayenne pepper, or to taste

½ teaspoon dried whole basil

1½ tablespoons fresh lemon juice

⅓ cup dry red wine

1½ cups seafood stock

2½ lbs redfish filets

In a large skillet over a medium-high heat make a medium colored roux with the oil and flour. This will take about 20–25 minutes and the roux will be thick. Add onions, green onion tops, bell pepper, garlic and celery to the hot roux. Cook for another 10 minutes stirring occassionally. Transfer the contents of the skillet to the slow cooker.

Add all other ingredients except the fish. Stir well and cook on high for 3 hours. Scrape the sides of slow cooker and mix sauce well. Cut the redfish into strips 3 to 4 inches wide. Place in slow cooker and cook on high for another 15 minutes.

Serve over steamed brown rice or mashed potatoes.

• •

Chef's Notes: *Redfish and Drum are, for culinary purposes, essentially the same fish and can substituted for each other in any recipe. If red-*

fish and drum are unavailable, use some other variety of mild flavored, white fleshed fish.

If you have concerns about making a roux, check out www.joesimmer.com or Joe Simmer's CREOLE Slow Cookin'.

● ●

WINE SUGGESTION: Any Reisling would complement this dish, and if you are in the mood for red, choose a lighter-bodied Zinfandel, an Australian Shiraz or Côtes du Rhône.

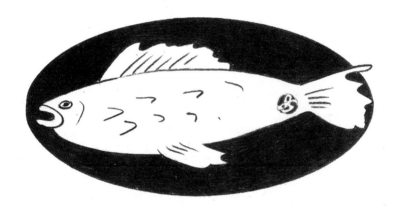

Bouillabaisse

SERVES 6

- 2 tablespoons extra virgin olive oil
- 1 large leek, white and light green parts, cut in half lengthwise and sliced into ¼ inch half-circles
- 1 large fennel bulb, quartered and thinly sliced
- 1 cup diagonally sliced celery, ¼ inch thick
- ½ cup minced shallot
- 1 bay leaf, crushed
- ½ teaspoon saffron threads
- 1 teaspoon salt, or to taste
- ¼ teaspoon cayenne pepper, or to taste
- 1 tablespoon minced garlic
- 1 tablespoon tomato paste
- 2 cups seafood stock (page 41) or bottled clam juice
- 1 14½ ounce can diced tomatoes with juice
- 1 lb firm white fish such as mahi-mahi, halibut, sea bass or red snapper, cut into 2 inch pieces
- 18 sea scallops (about ¾ lb)
- 18 medium to large peeled, butterflied shrimp, tail left on if desired (about ¾ lb)
- 1 tablespoon Pernod or Herbsaint
- 3 tablespoons chopped parsley

Heat the olive oil in a large skillet set over a medium heat. Add the sliced leek, fennel, celery, minced shallot, bay leaf, saffron threads, salt and cayenne pepper and sauté, stirring often until softened, but not browned. Stir in the minced garlic and tomato paste and cook for another minute or two. Transfer the contents of the pan to the crock, add the seafood stock and diced tomatoes and cook on high for 1½–2 hours or low for 3–4 hours.

If cooking on low, switch to high. Add the fish, scallops and shrimp, cover and cook for 30 minutes, or until seafood is cooked through. Gently stir in the Pernod or Herbsaint and parsley. Serve in large soup plates with whole wheat croutons and rouille, if desired (recipe follows).

• •

Chef's Notes: *Substitute shucked oysters or shelled mussels for the sea scallops; or for a very luxurious touch, add ½ pound or more jumbo lump crabmeat right before serving. The varieties of seafood used are less important than that they be high quality and very fresh.*

• •

WINE SUGGESTION: A Sancerre would be classic, but any Sauvignon Blanc or even an oddball white Bordeaux would swim. Steer away from oaky California or Australian Chardonnays.

Rouille

ROUILLE IS A SPICY, garlicky, mayonnaise-like sauce and is traditionally spread on toasted bread rounds or croutons and served with bouillabaisse.

2 egg yolks

1 tablespoon pressed fresh
   garlic

½ teaspoon cayenne pepper,
   or to taste

¼ teaspoon saffron threads

1 cup extra virgin olive oil

½ teaspoon salt, or to taste

Combine the egg yolks, garlic, cayenne and saffron in a mixing bowl and beat with a wire whip until well blended. Slowly drizzle in the olive oil while beating with the whip, until thickened. Add salt to taste. Refrigerate if you are not using it right away, and if it gets too thick, thin with warm water.

Curried Shrimp

2 tablespoons extra virgin olive oil

½ teaspoon Thai red chili paste, or to taste

2 cups chopped onions

2 tablespoons chopped garlic

1 cup chopped red or yellow bell pepper

¼ cup water.

½ cups seafood stock (page 41)

3 tablespoons natural peanut butter

1 tablespoon powdered dried shrimp

1 teaspoon salt

1 teaspoon ground black pepper

1 tablespoon grated fresh ginger

¼ teaspoon ground cloves

1½ tablespoons curry powder

4 lbs medium shrimp, peeled

1 medium sized unpeeled apple, cut into ½-inch chunks

1 tablespoon chopped fresh cilantro

½ cup golden raisins

¼ cup green onion tops, cut into 1-inch strips

Heat the olive oil in a large skillet over a high heat. When heated, whisk in the chili paste and blend well. Add the onions, garlic and bell pepper and stir-fry for 10 minutes.

Transfer contents of skillet to the slow cooker. Deglaze the skillet with the water. When reduced to half add to slow cooker. Add seafood stock, peanut butter, shrimp powder, salt, pepper, ginger and cloves. Stir together and cook on low for 4 hours. Add the shrimp, apple. cilantro, raisins and green onion tops. Cook for an additional 45 minutes on low. Serve over steamed brown rice in a bowl with crunchy, whole grain French bread.

Shrimp in Orange Sauce

2 tablespoons extra virgin olive oil

2 cups chopped onion

2 tablespoons chopped garlic

½ cup seafood stock (page 41) or chicken stock (page 40), or broth

1 tablespoon minced fresh ginger

1 tablespoon powdered dried shrimp

1 teaspoon salt

½ teaspoon ground black pepper

1 cup chopped red or yellow bell pepper

2 tablespoons grated orange peel

½ cup orange juice, with some pulp

1 tablespoon reduced sodium soy sauce

½ teaspoon Thai red chili paste

4 lbs medium size shrimp, peeled

1 tablespoon chopped fresh cilantro

Chopped fresh cilantro or green onion tops

Heat the olive oil in a large skillet on a medium-high heat. Saute the onions and garlic for 10 minutes or until soft. Transfer to slow cooker.

Add the stock, ginger, powdered dried shrimp, salt, pepper, bell pepper, orange peel, orange juice, soy sauce and chili paste to slow cooker. Cook on high for 2½ hours. Add shrimp and cilantro and cook for an additional 30 minutes. Serve over steamed brown rice in a bowl with crunchy, whole grain French bread for dipping. Garnish with chopped cilantro or chopped green onions tops.

Seafood Okra Gumbo

SERVES 6–8

HEALTHY GUMBO? This typical New Orleans home-style gumbo was always made in the summer, when okra, tomatoes, shrimp and crabs were plentiful. It's full of high-fiber vegetables and lean protein, low in saturated fat and devoid of refined carbohydrate. There's no roux and lots of okra, so it is much lighter than a Cajun style gumbo and most restaurant gumbos.

- **2 pounds sliced okra, fresh or frozen**
- **2 tablespoons balsamic vinegar**
- **¼ cup extra virgin olive oil**
- **3 cups chopped onion**
- **1 cup celery**
- **½ cup chopped bell pepper**
- **1 tablespoon minced garlic**
- **1 teaspoon salt, or to taste**
- **1 teaspoon black pepper**
- **½ teaspoon white pepper**
- **¼ teaspoon cayenne pepper**
- **1 teaspoon dried whole thyme**
- **3 bay leaves, crushed**
- **4 cups diced fresh tomato or 2—14½ ounce cans diced tomato with juice**
- **½ pound cleaned gumbo crabs, feelers removed**
- **1 pound medium-sized peeled shrimp**
- **4 cups seafood stock (page 41), or chicken stock (page 40), or low-sodium chicken broth**
- **1 pound claw or lump crabmeat**

Place the sliced okra in the crock and sprinkle on the balsamic vinegar. Heat the olive oil over a medium-high heat in a large skillet. Add the chopped onion, celery and bell pepper and cook, stirring occasionally, for about 15 minutes or until lightly browned. Stir in the garlic, salt, peppers, thyme and bay leaves and cook for 1 minute. Add the diced tomato and cook an additional minute, then transfer the contents of the pan to the slow cooker.

Break the gumbo crabs in half, break off the claws and add all to the crock, along with the peeled shrimp. Stir in the stock, cover and cook on high for 3½ hours or low for 6–7 hours. Gently stir in the crabmeat and cook for an additional 15 minutes on high or 30 minutes on low.

Serve over Louisiana Wild Pecan Rice or brown basmati rice.

• •

Chef's Notes: *Claw crabmeat has good flavor, none of the almost invisible cartilage, and is less expensive than lump crabmeat, which offers the luxurious benefit of large lumps.*

• •

WINE SUGGESTION: Try a Sancerre, a New Zealand Sauvignon Blanc, or a lighter bodied Pinot Noir.

Poached Salmon
with Dilled Dijon Sauce

THIS RECIPE TAKES A RARE DETOUR FROM THE USUAL use of the slow cooker. Rather than an appliance appreciated for long, slow cooking, it is employed as a controlled simmering device for the perfect poaching of salmon. The easily whipped up sauce gives the dish a distinctly fancy-pants dimension.

Loaded with omega-3 fatty acids and high quality protein, salmon is a nutritional powerhouse, not to mention a taste treat. For optimum flavor and health benefits, look for wild-caught North Atlantic or Alaskan varieties.

1 cup dry white wine	1 tablespoon minced fresh dill
½ cup water	
1 small onion, sliced	**SAUCE:**
3 garlic cloves, smashed	½ cup Greek style 2% milk-fat
½ teaspoon salt	yogurt
1 teaspoon black peppercorns	2 tablespoons Dijon mustard
1 bay leaf, crushed	1 tablespoon fresh lemon juice
1 tablespoon fresh lemon juice	3 tablespoons minced fresh
4 6 ounce salmon filets	dill

Combine the wine, water, onion, garlic, salt, peppercorns and bay leaf in the slow cooker and cook on high for 30 minutes, or up to an hour longer if convenient.

Add the lemon juice, and artfully arrange the salmon filets in the poaching liquid, skin side down. Sprinkle on the minced fresh dill, cover and continue cooking on high for 30 minutes. Using a spatula, carefully lift the filets out of the poaching liquid and onto plates or a platter. Serve warm, or chilled, with or without sauce as desired.

SAUCE: Combine the yogurt, mustard, lemon juice and dill. Mix well and refrigerate for 30 minutes or longer. Spoon the chilled or room temperature sauce over poached salmon filets, which may be served chilled, warm or at room temperature.

• •

Chef's Notes: *The salmon filet should be at least an inch thick. If you prefer your salmon on the rare side, check it after 15 minutes.*

• •

WINE SUGGESTION: Pinot Noir is a classic salmon accompaniment, but with the dill, a nice, rich Chablis would be lovely.

Creole Stewed Shrimp

SERVES 5-6

ALSO KNOWN AS SHRIMP CREOLE OR SHRIMP STEW, variations of this dish show up all over New Orleans and other parts of the gulf south. This healthier version substitutes tomato paste for the usual oil/white flour roux as a thickener, yielding a lighter, yet deeply flavorful dish.

When shopping for shrimp, fresh is always best, and be sure to purchase wild caught, preferably Gulf of Mexico shrimp, which have a much better flavor than farm raised shrimp.

2 **tablespoons extra virgin olive oil**
1 **cup chopped onion**
1 **cup chopped shallot**
1 **cup chopped green bell pepper**
2 **cups diagonally sliced celery, about 1/4 inch thick**
1 **tablespoon minced garlic**
1 **teaspoon black pepper**
1/2 **teaspoon white pepper**
1/8 **teaspoon cayenne pepper, or to taste**

1/2 **teaspoon whole dried thyme**
1 **bay leaf, crushed**
1 **teaspoon salt, or to taste**
1/4 **cup tomato paste**
1 **14 1/2 ounce can diced tomato, including liquid**
1 **cup tomato sauce**
2 **lbs peeled shrimp, about 50-60 count**
1/2 **cup thinly sliced green onion**
1/4 **cup chopped parsley**

Heat the oil in a large skillet set over a medium-high heat. Add the chopped onion, chopped shallot, chopped bell pepper and sliced celery. Cook, stirring occasionally, for 10–12 minutes or until the onions start to brown a bit. Stir in the garlic, black pepper, white pepper, cayenne pepper, thyme, bay leaf, salt and tomato paste. Cook and stir for 3 minutes. Transfer the contents of the pan to the crock and stir in the diced tomatoes and tomato sauce. Cover and cook on high for 2–3 hours or low for 4–6 hours. Stir well, scraping off anything stuck to the sides of the crock and stirring it back into the sauce.

The sauce should be very thick at this point. Stir in the shrimp, green onion and parsley and continue cooking on high for ½ hour or low for 1 hour.

Serve over steamed brown rice.

● ●

Chef's Notes: *If you use frozen shrimp, make sure they are completely thawed and well drained before using.*

● ●

WINE SUGGESTION: A French Sancerre or a California Sauvignon Blanc, or if you want red, the all-purpose Pinot Noir would be enjoyable.

Red Snapper Veracruz

ACCORDING TO JOE'S GREAT, GREAT UNCLE and legendary mariner Mathew Bloomfield Simmer, about a century or so ago a trade triangle thrived among the ports of New Orleans, Louisiana, Havana, Cuba and Veracruz, Mexico. Mathew kept a log of his travels with entries describing every meal he had eaten from the time he was sixteen until his death at age eighty-three, about an hour and a half after a large lunch of Seafood Gumbo, Frijoles Negros (Black Beans) and Pulpo Al Ajillo (Octopus in Garlic Sauce). This old family recipe comes from his diary.

1½ lbs fresh red snapper, cut into 4 pieces
1 teaspoon mild chili powder
½ teaspoon salt
1 tablespoon fresh lemon or lime juice
2 tablespoon extra virgin olive oil
1 large onion, cut in half and thinly sliced
1 medium poblano pepper or green bell pepper, cut in half and thinly sliced
2 tablespoons minced garlic

2 tablespoons minced fresh jalapeño pepper, or to taste
1 teaspoon dried oregano
3 bay leaves, crushed
½ teaspoon ground black pepper
2 tablespoons drained capers
½ cup coarsely chopped pitted green olives
1 14½ ounce can stewed tomatoes, including the liquid

Sprinkle the chili powder, salt and lemon or lime juice on the fish, cover it and refrigerate while slow cooking the sauce.

Heat the olive oil in a large skillet set over a high heat. Add the sliced onion and poblano or bell pepper and sauté for 3–4 minutes, until wilted. Stir in the garlic, jalapeño, oregano, bay leaves and black pepper and cook for another minute or two. Transfer the contents of the pan to the crock along with the capers, olives and tomatoes. Cover and cook on high for 1½–2 hours or low for 3–4 hours.

If cooking on low, switch to the high setting. Stir the sauce and adjust the seasoning. Add the marinated fish to the crock and spoon some of the sauce on top of each piece. Cover and cook for an additional 15–30 minutes, or until fish is done.

• •

Chef's Notes: *If snapper is unavailable, substitute redfish, speckled trout, grouper, mahi mahi, black drum or halibut, or any mild-to-medium flavored white fleshed fish.*

• •

WINE SUGGESTION: A Chablis from France, an un-oaked Chardonnay from California or Australia, or a Pinot Noir.

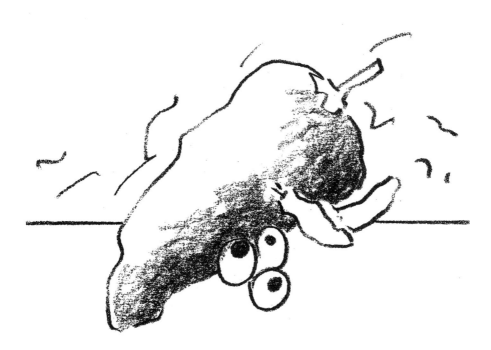

Chicken and Turkey

SKINLESS CHICKEN AND TURKEY are excellent sources of low fat protein, and both adapt well to the slow cooker. Look for all-natural, free-range birds raised without hormones and antibiotics. They taste better and are better for the body.

Chicken with Lemon and Olives
Chicken and Black Bean Chili
Jamaican Chicken
Turkey Meatballs and Spaghetti
Chicken Marengo
Turkey Meatloaf with Spinach
Smothered Okra, Tomatoes and Chicken
Chicken with Boiling Onions and Carrots
Chicken Cacciatore

Nutritional analysis available at
www.joesimmer.com,
courtesy of Corey C. Walsh, LDN, RD   **113**

Chicken with Lemon and Olives

SERVES 6–8

3 lbs skinless, boneless chicken thighs

½ cup whole wheat pastry flour

1 teaspoon salt

½ teaspoon ground black pepper

2 tablespoons extra virgin olive oil

1½ large lemons, sliced ¼-inch thick

1 cup pitted green olives, sliced ⅛-inch thick

2 tablespoons chopped garlic

½ cup dry white wine

2 cups chicken stock (page 40) or broth

¼ chopped parsley

Remove excess fat from chicken thighs and cut into bite-sized pieces. Set aside. In a medium bowl whisk the flour together with the salt and pepper. Heat the olive oil in a large skillet over a medium-high heat. Dredge the chicken in the seasoned flour and quickly brown on both sides. Set the lightly browned chicken on paper towels to drain. Place the chicken and all other ingredients in the crock and stir to mix. Cover and cook on high for 2½–3 hours or low for 5–6 hours.

Serve over whole-wheat couscous.

• •

Chef's Notes: *Whenever browning chicken before slow cooking, be sure to brown it quickly, not allowing it to linger in the pan and cook through, which would result in over done chicken. An easy way to dredge the chicken in the seasoned whole wheat flour is to shake it all up in a large paper or plastic bag.*

• •

WINE SUGGESTION: A red or white Burgundy or a red Côtes du Rhône.

Chicken Chili with Black Beans

C hipotle chili powder is made from dried, smoked jalapeno peppers, and is therefore smoky and quite spicy. You can play with the ratio of chipotle chili powder to mild chili powder if you like—but be careful!

- **4 cups finely chopped purple onion**
- **2½ cups finely chopped poblano peppers (about 2 large peppers)**
- **2 tablespoons minced garlic**
- **3 lbs boneless, skinless chicken thighs, cut into ½ inch pieces**
- **1 tablespoon chipotle chili powder**
- **2 tablespoons mild chili powder**
- **1½ teaspoon cumin**
- **1 teaspoon salt**
- **1 teaspoon whole dried oregano**
- **¼ cup chicken stock (page 40) or broth**
- **2 14 ounce cans black beans, drained**
- **½ cup thinly sliced green onions (optional)**

Combine the first 10 ingredients in the crock and stir to mix. Cover and cook on high for 3–4 hours or low for 6–8 hours. Stir and adjust the seasoning. Using the back of a cooking spoon, break up the chicken pieces a bit, and stir in the black beans. Cover and cook an additional ½ hour on high or 1 hour on low.

Serve in bowls garnished with sliced green onion, if desired.

• •

Chef's Notes: *This also makes a great taco filling. Use whole grain tortillas and garnish with diced fresh tomato, shredded lettuce or cabbage, sliced jalapeño, chopped cilantro, a squeeze of lime juice, etc.*

• •

Jamaican Chicken

SERVES 6

BACK IN THE DAY, Joe's friend Pete McIntosh's aunt owned and operated a "head" shop in an old building in New Orleans' French Quarter, selling all sorts of paraphernalia - pipes, papers, books, incense, occult items, hookahs and other earthly delights. When the building was sold last year (to be renovated into a fancy-pants boutique with two luxury condos upstairs), Joe helped Pete clean out the old shop's storeroom. Rummaging through a dusty cabinet, Joe found an old Rastafarian cookbook nestled between a case of outdated Chakra cream and some slightly used voodoo candles. He had great results with several of the recipes for baked items, but here is one he thought would translate well to the slow cooker. Although Jamaica is not particularly known for its cuisine, in a certain "Jamaican state of mind", this may be the most delicious thing you have ever eaten in your life.

9 chicken thighs, about 3 lbs	**2 tablespoons minced ginger**
1 teaspoon allspice	**1 scotch bonnet pepper, seeds**
¼ teaspoon cinnamon	**and membranes removed,**
¼ teaspoon nutmeg	**minced (optional)**
½ teaspoon black pepper	**½ cup chicken stock (page 40)**
1½ teaspoons thyme	**2 tablespoons soy sauce**
2 tablespoons dry mustard	**2 tablespoons balsamic**
1 tablespoon raw sugar	**vinegar**
1¼ teaspoons salt, or to taste	**2 tablespoons fresh lime juice**
2½ cups chopped onion	**1 teaspoon grated lime zest**
1 lb fresh yams, peeled and	**2 bay leaves**
cut into ½ inch dice	**2 cups sliced green onion**
1 tablespoon minced garlic	

Remove the skin from the thighs and trim off any visible fat, leaving the bone in. Rinse the thighs and pat dry. With a large, heavy chef knife or a meat cleaver, cut the thighs in half. Combine the next 8 ingredients in a small bowl. Season the thigh halves with the mixture, coating all sides, and place them in a bowl, cover and refrigerate for at least ½ hour or as long as overnight.

Combine the chopped onion, diced yams, minced garlic, ginger, scotch bonnet pepper, chicken stock, soy sauce, balsamic vinegar, lime juice, lime zest and bay leaves in the crock and stir to mix. Lay the seasoned chicken on top and sprinkle the sliced green onion over all. Cover and cook on high for 3–4 hours or low for 6–8 hours or until chicken is done and yams are tender.

Serve over steamed brown basmati rice, if desired.

Chef's Notes: *Scotch bonnet peppers are the same as habanero chiles and are one of the hottest peppers in all of creation. Use with care.*

WINE SUGGESTION: The slight sweetness of a German Riesling or Gewürztraminer would be an appropriate foil for the spiciness of this dish, or have a cold ginger beer.

Turkey Meatballs and Spaghetti

SERVES 6

JOE'S CHILDHOOD FRIEND Manny "Lil' Sausage" Mancuso's grandmother would roll over in her grave if she knew that that young Simmer boy was making her prized meatball recipe with ground turkey instead of her blend of pork and beef—that would be until she had a taste.

1½ lbs ground turkey breast
   or thigh, or a combination
   of the two
½–¼ cups dry whole wheat
   bread crumbs
½ cup finely chopped onion
½ cup finely chopped celery
1 tablespoon minced garlic
½ cup chopped fresh basil
1 egg, lightly beaten
1 teaspoon black pepper
⅛ teaspoon cayenne pepper

1 teaspoon salt
2 teaspoons olive oil
4 cups Thick and Chunky
   Tomato Sauce (page 38), or
   Creole Italian Red Gravy
   from *Joe Simmer's* CREOLE
   Slow Cookin', or your
   favorite tomato sauce
1 lb good quality whole
   grain spaghetti
   Shredded fresh basil for
   garnish (optional)

Pre-heat the oven to 400°. While the oven is heating, combine the ground turkey, bread crumbs, finely chopped onion and celery, garlic, basil, lightly beaten egg, black pepper, cayenne pepper and salt in a large bowl and mix well. Shape the mixture into 12—2-inch meatballs. Lightly oil a cookie sheet or flat baking pan with some of the olive oil. Using your hands, coat each ball with a bit of the oil and place them on the pan, being careful not to let them touch each other. Bake for 10 minutes.

Pour 2 cups of the tomato sauce or red gravy into the slow cooker. Gently position all the balls in the crock. Top with the remaining 2 cups of sauce. Cover and cook on high for 2–3 hours or low for 4–6 hours, or until a meat thermometer inserted into the center of a meatball reads at least 165°.

Prepare the spaghetti according to package directions. Serve just as you would serve normal meatballs and spaghetti.

Garnish with shredded fresh basil, if desired.

• •

Chef's Notes: *Ground turkey breast is leaner, but yields a slightly drier meatball than ground thigh. Ground turkey thigh is a little bit higher in fat content (but still a lot less than beef), and has a deeper flavor than ground turkey breast.*

• •

WINE SUGGESTION: Try a Chianti Classico, a California Sangiovese or a Cabernet Sauvignon. For white, go with a full bodied Chardonnay.

Chicken Marengo

SERVES 6

OTHER THAN STRAINED GREETINGS at family weddings and funerals, Joe hadn't spoken to his aunt Selma in years—ever since she gave him a D- on his final essay for gross misuse of metaphors. One of his mother's older sisters, Selma was a spinster English teacher, and led an orderly, disciplined existence. Their refusal to speak caused great tension at family gatherings.

Since then there's been a lot of water under that burned bridge, and Joe decided to do some fence mending. Now, as an accomplished author, he realized one poor grade was no big deal, and he decided he would bring the molehill to Mohammed, so to speak. He would bring Aunt Selma a peace offering. But what if she would not agree to let bygones be bygones? He could always blackmail her with the skeletons in her cloak room—rumors of her sadistic streak and penchant for necrophilia and bestiality—but that would, of course, be beating a dead horse. Rather than let the cat out of the bag, he decided to bury the hatchet and take the high road. Joe bit the bullet and brought Aunt Selma a big pot of slow cooked Chicken Marengo. Surprised, touched and thrilled, she declared to the family she would cross the Rubicon for Joe.

- 6 chicken leg quarters
- 1 tablespoon balsamic vinegar
- 1 tablespoon extra virgin olive oil
- 4 cups onion, cut in half length-wise, and sliced into half-circles
- 18 garlic cloves, peeled
- 9 small fresh Roma tomatoes, cut in half length-wise, peeled if desired
- 1 14½ ounce can quartered artichoke hearts, drained and rinsed
- 18 pitted Kalamata olives
- ½ cup white wine
- 1 tablespoons minced fresh rosemary
- 1 teaspoon dried thyme
- ½ teaspoon salt
- ½ teaspoon black pepper
- ½ cup chopped fresh parsley

Remove the skin and any visible fat from the chicken. Rinse and pat dry. Rub the balsamic vinegar into the chicken quarters and set aside.

Heat the olive oil in a large skillet over a medium-high heat. Add the onion half-circles and cook, stirring often for 8–10 minutes or until lightly browned. Add the whole peeled garlic cloves and the tomato halves and cook for another 3 minutes, stirring once or twice. Remove the pan from the heat.

Place the artichoke hearts and olives in the crock along with the contents of the skillet. De-glaze the skillet with the wine, add it to the crock and stir to mix. Arrange the chicken quarters on top. Combine the rosemary, thyme, salt and pepper in a small bowl and sprinkle the mixture over the chicken. Cover and cook on high for 2–3 hours or low 4–6 hours.

Remove the chicken quarters to a serving platter. Add the chopped parsley to the crock and stir to mix. Using a slotted spoon, distribute the solids from the crock onto the chicken quarters. Pour the liquid into a skillet and reduce over a high heat until desired consistency, then pour it over the chicken and vegetables.

• •

Chef's Notes: *The more you reduce a sauce or stock, the more intense the flavor becomes. It's a great way to thicken a sauce or gravy without using flour or cornstarch.*

• •

WINE SUGGESTION: Try a crisp Italian Pinot Grigio or a French Sancerre. If you are in the mood for red, have a Côtes du Rhône or Sangiovese.

Turkey Meatloaf with Spinach

SERVES 6–8

HIGH IN PROTEIN, LOW IN FAT and a dollop of l-tryptophan makes turkey a better choice than beef for preparing this satisfying comfort food. Oven cooked turkey meatloaves run the risk of being dry, due to the low fat content. This is not a problem in the slow cooker, as the moist heat keeps it juicy. Joe likes to use ground thigh meat for the flavor, but ground turkey breast, which is a little lower in fat, will work too.

2 **tablespoons extra virgin olive oil**

3 **cups chopped onion**

1 **small fennel bulb, finely chopped, about 2 cups**

1 **tablespoon minced garlic**

2 **teaspoons dried whole basil**

1 **teaspoon dried whole oregano**

2 **teaspoons black pepper**

¼ **teaspoon cayenne pepper**

1 **teaspoon salt, or to taste**

2 **lbs ground turkey thigh**

2 **eggs, lightly beaten**

¾ **cup dry whole wheat bread crumbs**

5 **ounces coarsely chopped fresh spinach, about 3–4 cups**

1 **cup tomato sauce**

Heat the olive oil in a large skillet. Add the chopped onion and fennel and cook over a medium high heat for 6–8 minutes, stirring often until softened. Stir in the minced garlic, basil, oregano, peppers and salt and cook for one more minute. Set aside.

Tear off a sheet of aluminum foil about 30 inches long and fold it in half to make a double-thick rectangle about 12 inches by 15 inches. Use the foil to line the bottom and sides of the crock. The two ends of the sheet running up the sides of the crock will allow you to easily lift the meatloaf out after it is done.

Combine the ground turkey, beaten eggs, breadcrumbs and spinach in a mixing bowl. Add the contents of the skillet to the bowl and mix well.

Form an oval shaped loaf and place it in the foil-lined crock. Spread the tomato sauce on top. Cook on high for 2½–3½ hours or low for 5–7 hours, or until a meat thermometer inserted in the center of the loaf reads 165 degrees. Remove the loaf by carefully pulling up on the ends of the foil extending up the sides of the crock. Allow any liquid or grease to drain off, and slide the loaf onto a serving platter. Sometimes turkey juices percolate to the top, through the tomato sauce, and congeal, sporting a freaky pinkish color. It is easily scraped off, revealing the rich hue of the underlying tomato sauce.

• •

Chef's Notes: *The onion, fennel, spinach and whole wheat bread crumbs provide a good amount fiber in this loaf. If you don't like the taste of fennel, substitute an equal amount of chopped celery. For a hyper-healthier version, replace ¼ to ½ cup of the breadcrumbs with an equal amount of oat bran, wheat bran or freshly ground flax seeds. All three add additional fiber, and the flax seed contributes a dose of omega-3 fatty acids.*

• •

WINE SUGGESTION: "A jug of wine, a loaf of turkey, a book of recipes, and thou." Joe's romantic instincts compel him to forgo the jug wine and spring for a nice Chianti when pitching the woo over a candlelit turkey meatloaf dinner.

Smothered Okra, Tomatoes and Chicken

JOE'S SECOND COUSIN PURVIS MC SIMMS (Joe's father's cousin Joe Mc Simms' boy) lived in his own doublewide on the family farm up in Mississippi, where he tended the hogs and worked on getting his GED. Never a particularly healthy eater, his lunch usually included a bacon cheeseburger or a Vienna sausage sandwich, a cream soda, and something packaged for dessert. Dinner invariably involved using one or more of his counter-top deep fat fryers. Purvis liked to hunt, and enjoyed frying and eating almost every part of the feral pigs he bagged.

One Wednesday afternoon while relaxing on his new plaid sectional sofa, watching cartoons and loading clips (and reviewing his algebra lesson), he felt some constriction and pressure in his chest. Thinking it was just a little indigestion brought on by his Slim Jim and Twinkie snack, he waited through two more episodes of Yosemite Sam before calling his paw and getting over to the Tallahatchie County emergency room. Upon hearing the words "mild heart attack", his whole life flashed through his mind, including his neighbor Nadine mentioning that cousin Joe was working on a healthy cookbook. Purvis called Joe the next morning, embraced the healthy slow-cookin' concept, and took a particular shinin' to this recipe.

1½ lbs boneless, skinless chicken thighs cut into bite-sized pieces
1 teaspoon salt, or to taste
1 teaspoon black pepper
½ teaspoon white pepper
⅛ teaspoon cayenne pepper
½ teaspoon thyme
½ teaspoon basil
2 tablespoon extra virgin olive oil, divided
¼ pound turkey bacon
3 cups chopped onion
½ cup chopped green bell pepper
½ cup chopped celery
1 bay leaf, crushed
½ teaspoon Tabasco sauce, or to taste
2 pounds sliced okra, fresh or frozen
2 tablespoons balsamic vinegar
2 cups diced fresh tomato, or 1—14½ ounce can diced tomatoes, with liquid

Cut the chicken thighs into bite-sized chunks, removing any visible fat. Combine the salt, black pepper, white pepper, cayenne, thyme and basil in a small bowl. Sprinkle it over the chicken chunks and toss to evenly distribute. Set aside.

Heat 1 tablespoon of the olive oil in a large skillet set over a medium-high heat. Add the turkey bacon and cook, turning occasionally, until browned and crisp. Set aside on paper towels to drain and cool.

Heat the other tablespoon of olive oil to the pan and add the chopped onion, bell pepper and celery. Continue cooking on medium-high, stirring occasionally, until tender and a little bit browned—about 12 minutes. Stir in the bay leaf and Tabasco and remove the pan from the heat.

Place the okra in the slow-cooker. Sprinkle on the balsamic vinegar and add the tomatoes. Crumble or chop the turkey bacon and add it to the crock. Transfer the contents of the skillet and the seasoned chicken chunks to the crock and stir to mix. Cover and cook on high for 2–3 hours or low for 4–6 hours.

• •

Chef's Notes: *Turkey bacon has come a long way since it was first introduced. While it is not a dead ringer for the real thing, it is very good for seasoning dishes such as this, and contains no saturated fat, 75% less total fat, half the calories and 3 times the protein of pig bacon. Look for an uncured, all-natural brand without added nitrites.*

• •

WINE SUGGESTION: Something light and crisp, such as a California Sauvignon Blanc, or perhaps a rosé from the Rhone valley.

Ode to Joe

by Nadine

I'll never forget
That day on the pond
Row, Joe, Row

You were so strong
I was so blond
Go, Joe, Go

My clothes got so rumpled
My hair was a mess
Slow, Joe, Slow

I sometimes said no
I always meant yes
No, Joe, No

Until you return
I'll wear a black dress
Mo', Joe, Mo'

Chicken with Boiling Onions and Carrots

SERVES 6–8

2 lbs skinless, boneless chicken thighs

½ cup whole-wheat pastry flour

1 teaspoon salt

1 teaspoon ground black pepper

2 tablespoons extra virgin olive oil

1 lb boiler onions, skin removed

1 lb carrots, cut into ½ inch slices

2 cups chicken stock (page 40) or broth

½ teaspoon whole dried thyme

4 3 or 4 inch sprigs fresh rosemary

Remove excess fat from chicken thighs and cut into bite-sized pieces and set aside. In a medium bowl whisk the flour together with the salt and pepper. Heat the olive oil in a large skillet set over a medium-high heat. Dredge the chicken in the seasoned flour and quickly brown on both sides. Drain the lightly browned chicken pieces on paper towels.

Remove skin from boiler onions by plunging them into boiling water for 30 seconds, then remove and peel.

Place the chicken, onions and all other ingredients in the crock, cover and cook on high for 3–3½ hours or low for 6–7 hours.

Serve over steamed brown rice or in bowl with crunchy whole-grain bread for dipping.

• •

Chef's Notes: *An easy way to "dredge" the chicken is to put the seasoned flour in a paper or plastic bag, add the chicken and shake the bag.*

• •

WINE SUGGESTION: The universal wine food, chicken, goes well with the universal food wines, Pinot Noir or Chardonnay.

Chicken Cacciatore

ALWAYS VERY APPEARANCE CONSCIOUS, Joe's twenty-something niece Jocelyn worked as a personal trainer at the Texas Riviera Health Spa and Salon outside Houston. She worked out like crazy—aerobics, weight machines, Pilates, spinning classes, power yoga—and lived on protein powder shakes, bio-enhanced bottled water and energy drinks. And she took much too much advantage of her unlimited free use of the salon's tanning bed. Fit, buff and bronzed, her overall look was that of a thin slice of crisp bacon.

After a full summer of this regimen, she found herself feeling fatigued often, and nervous always, with fits of yawns interrupting her constant chatter about weight loss, clothes, celebrities and relationship problems. She called uncle Joe for some advice. Concerned and amused, Joe convinced her to substitute a weekly spray on tan session for the tanning bed, and put her on a diet of healthy, natural, slow-cooked food. Under Joe's avuncular tutelage, Jocelyn was able to maintain her appearance and social standing, while being able to relax and "feel good about her self". She particularly enjoyed this healthy recipe.

- 6 boneless, skinless chicken breasts, about 2½ pounds
- ½ teaspoon salt
- 1 teaspoon black pepper
- 1 tablespoon fresh rosemary, minced
- 2 teaspoons dried whole basil
- 1 teaspoon dried whole oregano
- 1 tablespoon extra virgin olive oil
- 3 cups chopped onion
- 1 cup sliced celery
- 2 tablespoons minced garlic
- 2 tablespoons tomato paste
- 3 bay leaves, crushed
- 1 14½ ounce can diced tomatoes
- ½ cup dry red wine
- 6 ounces baby Portabella mushrooms, cleaned, trimmed and cut into quarters
- ¼ cup chopped fresh parsley or basil, (optional)

Trim any visible fat from the chicken breasts. Combine the salt, pepper, rosemary, basil and oregano in a small bowl. Rub the mixture into both sides of the chicken breasts and set aside.

Heat the olive oil in a large skillet set over a medium-high heat. Add the chopped onion and sliced celery and cook, stirring occasionally, until tender and a little bit browned—about 12 minutes. Stir in the garlic, tomato paste and bay leaves and cook 3 more minutes. Remove the pan from the heat and stir in the diced tomatoes, including any liquid in the can, and the red wine.

Place the mushrooms into the crock. Distribute about half the contents of the skillet over the mushrooms, and then arrange the seasoned chicken breasts on top. Spread the remaining contents on the skillet over the chicken breasts. Cover and cook on high for 2–2½ hours or low for 4–5 hours. Stir in the chopped fresh parsley or basil, if desired.

• •

Chef's Notes: *Buy the "toothpaste tubes" of tomato paste, available at most supermarkets and Italian specialty stores. They last for months in the refrigerator, and you can use just a tablespoon or so without wasting the rest. Those tubes can also be a great prank when placed in your guest bathroom after a large night out.*

• •

WINE SUGGESTION: Lots of possibilities here. Most dry whites or light-to-medium bodied reds would pair nicely with this dish.

Shopping Guide

HEALTHY, ALL-NATURAL AND ORGANIC INGREDIENTS are much more available now than they were just a few years ago. Here's a non-exhaustive list of products and vendors:

Packaged broths: Swanson low-sodium Chicken Broth, Pacific Natural Foods Organic Chicken Broth and Organic Vegetable Broth, Imagine Foods Organic Chicken Stock, Organic Free Range Chicken Broth, Organic No-Chicken Broth and Organic Vegetable Broth.

Beans, Peas and Lentils: Camellia® dried beans, peas and lentils are a good grocery store brand with a pretty broad range of products. Another good source of dried legumes is the bulk department of natural grocery stores such as Whole Foods Market and Wild Oats Marketplace, where organically grown beans, peas and lentils are often available. There are also many on-line, mail order sources. Just use your favorite search engine to find the bean you are seeking.

Remember, the older the bean, the drier it is, and the longer it will take to cook. If the beans look cracked and the skin appears to be peeling off, it is probably too old. Look for dates on packaged products, and buy where you know there is a fast turnover of products.

Canned beans are widely available and generally very good quality. Look for all-natural varieties, or organic if you wish. Ingredients should include only beans, water and a little salt.

Whole Grains: As above, the bulk bins of natural grocery stores, and many supermarkets also carry whole wheat pastry flour, whole grain pastas, brown rice, barley and dried posole. Checking the internet is an easy way to find sources, both locations of stores and products available by mail. For example, entering "short grain brown rice" into a search engine will yield about 1,720,000 search results!

Tomato Products: Muir Glen Organic produces a line of organic tomato products including Diced Tomatoes, Tomato Sauce, Tomato Paste, and some of the fore mentioned in "no added salt" variations.

Del Monte now has a line of organic Diced Tomatoes, several with herbs and other seasonings.

365 Organic is a private label of Whole Foods Market.

Chicken and Turkey products: Natural grocery stores carry free-range, hormone and antibiotic free poultry. When shopping for chicken sausage, turkey sausage or smoked turkey, look for and all-natural brand without added nitrites, available at natural food stores and many supermarkets (Diestel is a good brand). Again, the internet is a very handy tool.

Sources: Joe likes to buy locally produced food. When that is not possible in your area, here are some reputable mail order operators:

Sun Organic Farm
www.sunorganicfarm.com
888-269-9888
Beans, peas, lentils, short grain brown rice and more

Fiddler's Green Farm
www.fiddlersgreenfarm.com
800-729-7935
Beans, peas, lentils, and more

Chef Shop
www.chefshop.com
800-596-0885
Beans, peas, lentils, and more

Bob's Red Mill
www.bobsredmill.com
800-349-2173

Pacific Natural Foods
www.pacificfoods.com
503-692-9666
Organic chicken and vegetable broths and more

Murray's Chickens
www.murrayschicken.com
800-770-6347
All natural chicken products

Diestel Family Turkey Ranch

www.diestelturkey.com
888-446-2253
All natural turkey products

New Orleans Fish House

www.nofh.com
800-821-9700
Fresh and frozen shrimp, fish, crabmeat and more.

Savoie's Sausage and Food Products, Inc.

www.savoiesfoods.com
337-942-7241
Turkey Tasso

Whole Foods Market

www.wholefoodsmarket.com
A site loaded with healthy product information and an easy store locater.

Index

Notes to Self

Notes to Joe

Notes to Self

Notes to Joe

NOW IN PRINT

· ·

COMING SOON

ALL-AMERICAN
Summer 2008

ASIAN

HOLIDAY

MEDITERRANEAN

2 MARTINI PRESS, LLC
5500 Prytania Street
#616
New Orleans, LA 70115
www.2martinipress.com